WATERLOO

In The Footsteps of The Commanders

Jonathan Gillespie-Payne

Pen & Sword
MILITARY

First published in Great Britain in 2004 by
Pen & Sword Military
an imprint of
Pen & Sword Books Ltd
47 Church Street
Barnsley
South Yorkshire
S70 2AS

ISBN 1-84415-050-X

Typeset in Palatino

Printed and bound in Great Britain by CPI UK

For a complete list of Pen & Sword titles, please contact
Pen & Sword Books Limited
47 Church Street, Barnsley, South Yorkshire, S70 2AS, England
E-mail: enquiries@pen-and-sword.co.uk
Website: www.pen-and-sword.co.uk

CONTENTS

FOREWORD

Waterloo – In the footsteps of the Commanders is a fascinating guide to the Battle of Waterloo, providing great insight into the character and ability of the key protagonists. Wellington and Napoleon have been the subject of many biographies and their place in history has made them particularly well known – but how many people really know what influences guided their actions at Waterloo?

This book gets inside the minds of the Commanders, providing interesting and thought-provoking insights to the horror and chaos of the battlefield of Waterloo and the difficulty of commanding such large forces as they lock in close combat.

By focusing on the Commanders, Jonathan Gillespie-Payne has highlighted the differing personalities, their natural ability and military competence in the context of a most complex battle. The outcome of the Battle of Waterloo, which hung in the balance to the final hour, rested on the Commanders' decision-making under enormous pressure and without timely information on the enemy's future intentions. This was a battle won by the discipline and the stubborn determination of the Infantry. Almost half of the Infantry Officers present were either killed or wounded. In the case of the 3rd Battalion The Royal Scots, four Officers and the Sergeant Major were killed whilst carrying the King's Colour alone.

The difficulties of command and control have been paramount in every battle throughout history from the earliest times to modern day combat with secure radio and data communications. This lively and exciting guide brings to life the reality of the Commanders' responsibility and the impact of their leadership on the lives of some 200,000 individuals on the battlefield.

While the dedicated military historian will be stimulated by Jonathan Gillespie-Payne's analysis, this guide will be easily assimilated by those with little knowledge of warfare. It has been particularly pleasant for me to see one of the young officers who served with me when I commanded the 1st Battalion The Royal Scots in Germany in the mid-1980s tackle such a complicated subject with such clarity. He had a flair for military history then which is so evident in this guide, Jonathan's first book; *Waterloo – In The Footsteps Of The Commanders'* is an outstanding read for the expert and lay person alike.

MAJOR GENERAL MARK STRUDWICK CBE, THE CASTLE, EDINBURGH

INTRODUCTION

Ever since I was a young boy, I have held an untamed curiosity for the events of 18 June 1815. Initially it was the splendour of the Napoleonic era, the uniforms, the romance, but as I have grown older, I have been captivated by the personalities and how they interacted. As a former soldier, and one who has known that gut-wrenching fear the individual feels when they face battle for the first time, the ability of the soldiers to withstand what they did that day is almost unfathomable. It was, therefore, only logical that one of the first ports of call when I went to live in Brussels for two years would be the battlefield at Waterloo.

I was bitterly disappointed when I first visited. The Belgians had built a huge memorial to the Prince of Orange and in the process had destroyed the sunken road and turned the centre of the Allied line around this monument into a cheap and tacky tourist trap selling expensive and shabby tourist trinkets. I can only agree with the Duke of Wellington when he declared after visiting Waterloo in the 1820's that 'they have spoilt my battlefield'. I looked to buy a guide, one that was compact, readable, contained enough detail to satisfy my curiosity but not too much to bog me down and detract from my tour of the battlefield. The only guide I could find in English was evidently aimed at bus groups and had nowhere near the information I wanted or indeed already knew, so I decided to tour the battlefield alone with only my own knowledge.

By the end of the day, I was stunned and found myself asking who had won the battle anyway? The local preference for Napoleon was so strong, anyone who visited the place without prior knowledge would have assumed a French victory and assumed that this bloody field was the reason why the nations of Europe have come together to form a community that will eventually become one enormous common identity. Belgian self-promotion? Wounded French pride justifying defeat? British reserve unable to 'blow one's own trumpet'?

I decided at that point the battlefield deserved a guide book, not only one that accurately placed, translated and explained the many memorials, explained the events of the battle both on 18 June and also in the greater context, but also took on a more personal angle. What exactly did the commanders see that day? The valley between the opposing armies must have been a dark, smoke-filled hell hole choked with blood and torn bodies and certainly would not have provided the sort of views one sees today. And who were the commanders? Wellington and Napoleon surely; this was the title fight, the two greatest captains of their day meeting for the first time. But it wasn't that simple. Napoleon had given command of his Left Wing to Marshal Michel Ney, the most colourful and probably most maligned of all of Napoleon's twenty-six soldiers he promoted to the Marshalate. Ney was the French battle captain that day, responsible for the tactical handling of the army, leaving Napoleon to control the strategic level. It therefore makes sense to look at both Napoleon and Ney when touring the battle from the French command perspective. All three men were different; Wellington the consummate professional soldier, driven by duty; Napoleon the military genius whose ambition knew no bounds and Ney, the barrel cooper's son who rose from the ranks with a Marshals baton in his knapsack and sought only the sort of glory that a schoolboy dreams of.

The result of my wanderings around the battlefield of Waterloo is this book, yet another in the in a long line of books about the most written about battle in world history. It was written for a reason, born out of frustration because of the lack of specific material for my needs. It is compact, hopefully easy to read and contains just enough detail to appeal to both the enthusiast and the uninitiated. My wish is you come away from the battlefield with not only a clear understanding of what happened, but why it happened and why events ordered by the respective commanders unfolded. I believe this guide needed to be written to give that understanding and because when 50,000 men become casualties at the rate of just under 100 per minute, they deserve that understanding from future generations.

JGP
Farnham
December 2003

PART ONE
The Protagonists

This is a man with whom I shall have to deal

NAPOLEON, on hearing of Wellington's victory at Assaye, 1803

CHAPTER 1

'WE HAD A NOTION THAT WHILE HE WAS THERE NOTHING COULD GO WRONG'

LORD ROBERTS described Arthur Wellesley, Duke of Wellington as 'reserved, unsympathetic, perhaps a little selfish'. Born the second son of the Anglo-Irish Earl of Mornington in Ireland in 1769, his father died when he was a boy and received very little affection from his mother who did not know what 'I shall do with my ugly son Arthur'. After a brief spell at Eton, where the young Wellesley in his own words 'learnt nothing', he was packed off to Brussels and then the non-military French academy at Angers. Save for his fluent French, Arthur Wellesley was probably one of the least educated of his contemporaries when he became an Ensign in the 73rd Regiment of Foot in March 1787.

Through the system of purchased commissions it was not surprising, given his privileged background, that Wellesley rose rapidly through the ranks, serving in both infantry and cavalry regiments until he became the Lieutenant Colonel of the 33rd Regiment of Foot in 1793. Although he had still not heard a shot fired in anger, Wellesley was far from uneducated in the ways of the British Army. From the onset, he had taken great care to educate himself, firstly about the limits, strengths and weaknesses of the individual soldier and then how each grouping of troops could best function. In later life he would state that 'one must understand the mechanism and power of the individual soldier, then that of a company, or battalion, or brigade, and so on, before one can venture to group divisions or move an army'. Now, as the commander of a regiment, Wellesley would be given his opportunity to put all his hard won theory into practice during the Duke of York's disastrous campaign to Flanders in 1794. In the harrowing retreat that followed, Wellesley learnt in adversity 'what not to do, and that was always something'. Most importantly, he learnt how to handle a regiment, the importance of sound logistics and how to conduct a rearguard action, all lessons that would later be crucial to the success of the armies he commanded.

Having now been thoroughly grounded in the art of war at regimental level, Wellesley found himself and the 33rd bound to India in 1797. If his career was undistinguished up to this point, all was about to change. Arriving as a Lieutenant Colonel, he would rise by 1805 to the rank of Lieutenant General and the name Wellesley would be known not only throughout England but would have come to the attention of Napoleon himself. His elder brother, the Earl of Mornington, had assumed the role of Governor General and gave his sibling the opportunity to shine. This opportunity reached a climax at Assaye in 1803 when, outnumbered ten to one, Wellesley chose to attack and defeated the army of the Mahratta. The great General had finally arrived. Wellesley now had the experience of formation command and all his understanding of the army from the individual soldier upwards formed the basis of the successes that would follow against the armies of Napoleon, culminating at Waterloo.

Earl of Mornington

Wellesley was preparing to fight the Spanish in South America when Napoleon intervened, invaded Spain and turned England's enemy into England's ally. The war in the Iberian peninsular was to take Wellesley from well known but relatively unheralded 'Sepoy General' to the foremost soldier of his generation. Having served under better known if less competent generals during the early part of the Peninsular War, he was given command of the entire theatre in 1809. At Vimiero, he defeated Junot using similar tactics to those he would employ at Waterloo, defending a ridge, concealing his troops on the reverse slope and smashing French infantry columns with disciplined fire from troops in line. The Battle of Busaco followed a similar pattern; this time Masséna was the unfortunate French commander with Foy and

Arthur Wellesley, Duke of Wellington.

Wellington in command. By the time of Waterloo every French commander, except Napoleon, nursed a grudging respect for the 'Sepoy-General'.

Ney as subordinates. Victory followed victory in both offensive and defensive battles as well as successful withdrawals and the list of defeated French marshals and generals, including Soult, Reille, Marmont and d'Erlon grew more impressive. By the time the British were pushing into southern France, an army commanded by Arthur Wellesley was regarded with extreme caution by all French generals and marshals with the exception of Napoleon.

With the abdication and exile to Elba of the French emperor, the newly created Duke of Wellington now assumed his post as Ambassador to Paris. In England he was no longer the efficient but unheralded 'Sepoy General', but the saviour of Europe. He was regarded as a tough disciplinarian and has often been quoted out of context as having little regard for the men that he led. In truth, he was an aristocrat, an archconservative and probably lacked the common touch when dealing with the rank and file who, in turn, certainly lacked the finer qualities of Georgian gentility. There can be no doubt that he cared very much for the ordinary soldier, he abhorred waste of life and never took unnecessary risks with his soldiers' lives. They were always fed and supplied, he took personal issue with the administrators in England when pay was not getting through, and he knew what made his soldiers function. 'I found the English regiments in best humour when we were well supplied with beef; the Irish when we were in the wine countries; the Scotch when the dollars for pay came up. This looks like an epigram, but I assure you it was the fact, and quite perceptible'. By the time he crossed the Pyrenees 'there never was an army in the world in better spirits, better order, better discipline'. Wellington may have said off the record that the British soldier was 'the scum of the earth' but he also said he was 'a dependable article' and proud of the way they transformed into a disciplined fighting force.

His personal habits were those of a soldier rather than that of the gentry from which he came. He ate what his soldiers ate, much to the consternation of the Spanish officers who were attached to his Headquarters during the Peninsular War. Wellington was exceptionally fit in both mind and body; Napier described him as 'iron hardihood of body, a quick and sure vision, a grasping mind, untiring power of thought, and the habit of laborious minute investigation and arrangement'. He remained calm in a crisis and never became excited whatever the situation. After the storming of the fort at Ciudad Rodrigo, a soldier was dispatched to give Wellington the news and in his excitement announced that 'I have taken the fort, sir!' to which Wellington replied, 'Oh, you have taken the fort, have you? Well, I'm glad to hear it'. The qualities were mutually supporting and his uncanny ability to be in the right place at the right time and make correct decisions in a snap were only possible over a protracted period of time due to his superlative physical condition.

Wellington was highly respected by all ranks and social strata of those he led although he was not loved and feted in the same manner as Napoleon; Wellington despised any form of hero-worship and thought Napoleon not to be a gentleman because of it. Wellington was first and foremost a servant of his country, prepared to battle politicians for the benefit of his troops, but ultimately did as requested by his government. Napoleon, by contrast, was the State. Officers felt supreme confidence in Wellington's ability and 'had the notion that while he was there nothing could go wrong'; the soldiers adopted a simplistic view when 'Old Nosey' was in command. The soldier knew that Wellington would keep him well supplied, would not take unnecessary risks with his life and always defeated the French in battle. 'What more could a soldier ask for?' quipped one British Private.

The Anglo-Dutch army that Wellington commanded was not of the same quality as his British Peninsular force, indeed the Duke referred to it as 'infamous'. In 1814, much of the Peninsular Army had disbanded or sent to America and therefore most of the experienced soldiers were absent at Waterloo. Of the Duke's infantry, only one third was British or King's German Legion (KGL), soldiers whom he could trust, and of those only half were Peninsular veterans. Historians generally agree that the Duke was right to be wary of the other nationalities, especially the Dutch-Belgians who formed a third of his infantry force. Not only was their soldiering ability unpredictable, loyalty was a major concern; many Belgians had strong sympathies for Napoleon. In the event, some of these units performed heroically, others disgracefully. The Duke's cavalry and artillery comprised of over half British or KGL, but British cavalry at the time had a reputation for being brave and hard fighters, but prone to over excitement bordering on the uncontrollable. As the battle unfolded, the heavy cavalry were to prove this reputation accurate. The Anglo-Dutch army was therefore of untried and questionable ability, its main strengths lay in the discipline of its British and KGL veterans and the ability of its commander. Napoleon's confidence on the morning of the battle was due not so much that he was facing Wellington, who in public he ridiculed but in private he admired, but more so because he was not facing Wellington's Peninsular War army. Wellington, who had defeated every French General and Marshal that had been pitted against him, publicly admired Napoleon but privately expressed reservations over his handling of a field army, was quietly confident in his own ability to defeat the Emperor. When asked if he could beat the French, Wellington pointed at a British infantryman and said 'it all depends upon that article, give me enough of it and I am sure'.

CHAPTER 2

'THE NAPOLEON WE KNEW DOES NOT EXIST ANYMORE'

I LOVE POWER like a musician loves music' was how Napoleon described his own ambition and drive. He was born on 15 August 1769 on Corsica at a time when the island had just been ceded to France, his father submitted to French rule and gained some esteem in Paris because of it. His mother was made of sterner stuff and was 'without equal' in the eyes of the young Napoleon, influencing and moulding his character through her harsh disciplinary regime. Napoleon craved power and influence, and as Corsica was but a mere organ of France, it was to Paris that he began to see his future.

Through family contacts, Napoleon was awarded a scholarship at the French Military Academy but first required to learn the language. At the age of nine, he set foot in France for the first time, a loner, a Corsican and learning to despise the aristocracy that was to surround him for the next seven years of study.

Unlike Wellington, Napoleon was a determined scholar, always trying to improve himself. He had a natural ability with mathematics and cartography, but also read history, law and philosophy widely. Napoleon considered Britain to be a successful nation and set about studying how that success was attained, although he would appear to have missed the point about democracy. He was commissioned at the age of sixteen into a good artillery regiment where he began to learn his trade and developed his

Napoleon's mother was 'without equal' in her son's eyes.

belief in the overriding power of the field gun. He developed an admiration for the works of Rousseau and believed in the philosophy of equality and the abolition of privileges, but Bourbon France was not suited to this way of thinking. Indeed, Napoleon felt there was 'no place for myself in this world'. The French revolution that began in 1789 changed everything for Napoleon. Although wary of mob rule, he embraced the collapse of the Bourbon monarchy and saw opportunities for himself to gain in power and influence.

Napoleon returned briefly to Corsica in an attempt to enter politics and

Napoleon as an earnest and ambitious lieutenant of artillery.

lead the island of his birth, but he fell out with his allies, his family was declared traitors and forced back to France. Napoleon found his adopted country in political chaos with the constitution suspended and The Terror underway. Senior army officers, who were almost exclusively from the aristocracy, were leaving in droves and at a time when the nation was at war with Austria, Spain, Prussia and Britain. Although only a captain, the vacuum that was being generated in the senior ranks presented a situation that was ideal for Napoleon to come to the attention of those in Paris who really mattered. At Toulon, the population had rebelled against Paris and allowed the British to occupy the harbour. Napoleon was placed in command of the artillery of the force sent to bring Toulon back to heel. He identified the positions of key importance and persuaded the commander to allow him to capture and occupy the high positions surrounding the harbour. Napoleon brought his guns to bear from the heights and succeeded in driving the Royal Navy warships back into the open sea. Although not in command of the whole operation, he was given the public credit for his actions and within three months had become a brigadier.

With his star in the ascendancy, Napoleon was given his second big break in October 1795, when tasked with stopping the monarchist rebellion as it descended upon Paris. With unflinching brutality, Napoleon used 'a whiff of grapeshot' on the mob at close range, killing and maiming

Napoleon administers 'a whiff of grapeshot' to subdue the Royalist uprising, an act that secured the promotion to general at the age of twenty-six.

several hundred and dispersing the crowd thus ending the rebellion. Napoleon was now regarded as politically sound, and within three weeks he was promoted to general and given command of the Army of the Interior. He was only twenty-six years of age.

Ambition still drove him forward, he met and married Josephine; an aging socialite with important connections, and through her influence was given command of the army in Italy in 1796. Although an object of fun for older officers to whom he now was senior, Napoleon offered the soldiers spoils of war in return for hard fighting and always led by example. He demonstrated the strategy that he would take to Waterloo by splitting the Hapsburg and Piedmontese armies, defeating each in detail by fighting six battles inside two weeks, thereby destroying the Austrian influence in Italy. The soldiers idolised him, the generals admired him, Paris was wary of him and his reputation. Napoleon the soldier had finally arrived.

Napoleon's ambition was still driving him forward. He funded his own, ill-fated expedition to Egypt, but had the good sense to leave his army and return to Paris to ensure his reputation was untarnished. Relying on his public popularity, along with Abbe Sieyes and Roger Ducos, Napoleon overthrew the hated Directory in the Coup de Brumaire in November 1799, establishing a power-sharing triumvirate. Within months, Napoleon had eased the other two out of power, establishing himself as Premier Consul and effectively the leader of France.

Napoleon, in Hannibalesque style, crossed the Alps into Italy where the Austrian Hapsburgs were again gaining influence. Crushing his enemy at Marengo and Hohenlinden, he forced the

Napoleon crosses the Alps in an operation he compared to the feats of Hannibal.

Austrians to sue for peace. With no wars to fight, he now turned his attention to running France: 'we have done with the romance of the Revolution' he stated, 'we now must begin its history'. He brought the church back into mainstream society and introduced a new Civil Code; he was at the zenith of his power, popularity and influence, if not his boundless ambition and confidence. On 2 December 1804 he crowned himself Emperor.

Had Napoleon stopped at this juncture, he may well have survived and established a Bonaparte dynasty that would have served France for decades to come, but his ambition for greater power and his paranoia of losing what he had already achieved was to condemn him to the long road to Waterloo. Although Britain had always opposed Napoleon, the other powers in Europe had been beaten into submission, but, the needless kidnapping from neutral Baden, show trial and execution of the Royalist figurehead Duc d'Enghien led to the formation of the Third Coalition.

Apart from the short period of his exile in Elba, France was to know only war with its associated hardships from 1804 to 1815. Despite victories over the Austrians at Ulm and Austerlitz, Britain controlled the seas, making an invasion of his closest enemy impossible. Napoleon introduced the Continental System, baring Europe from trading with Britain, but Portugal refused. Napoleon sent an army through allied Spain to enforce his law and foolishly replaced the Spanish king, Charles IV, with his brother, Joseph Bonaparte. Through his own ambition to build a Bonaparte dynasty in Europe, he had committed France not only to war with the British and Portuguese in the Iberian peninsular, but had now turned the Spanish against him.

On 2 December 1804, Napoleon crowned himself as emperor and immediately created the Marshalate.

His divorce of Josephine and marriage to Marie-Louise of Austria was meant to cement peace between the two nations, but Austria found renewed confidence in British resistance and, along with Russia, again went to war with Napoleon,. This forced France to wage war on all fronts and slowly she was bled dry. The invasion of Russia in 1812 was a crushing disaster; defeated by the cold winter and lack of food, Napoleon retreated to France.

In 1813, Napoleon fought through Germany in an attempt to stop the Russians before he could turn his attention to defeating Wellington in the Peninsular. Prussia promptly turned on Napoleon and allied itself with Russia and Austria to form an overwhelming force that defeated Napoleon at Leipzig. With Wellington breaking out of Spain and into

In 1814, after fighting a brilliant defensive campaign, Napoleon was forced to abdicate and face exhile in Elba. Marshal Ney grips the Emperor's hand.

France itself and the European powers invading from the east, Napoleon fought a last-ditch campaign before being forced to abdicate and go to exile in Elba.

Napoleon was a self-made man from humble origins whose mother had instilled in him a sense of determination and a lust for power. Napoleon was not overly bothered where he found that power; he had toyed with the idea of joining the Royal Navy and considered fighting as a mercenary for Turkey. France was simply the nearest and easiest option and happened to be in the throws of revolution at the most convenient time. He was however a true military genius. He developed the concept of all-arms groupings and mission orientated orders that would be familiar to the modern soldier, had a remarkable grasp of logistics and was brilliant in the use of maps. Napoleon had an unshakable

Napoleon in campaigning uniform, complete with famous grey overcoat.

faith in the power of the cannon, believing it could instil fear into an enemy that would override its ability to fight when used in sufficient numbers. He was a 'high-risk, high-gain' battle-captain who was largely successful and spectacularly so. He used a simple strategy of divide and conquer, defeating his enemies in detail, something that was central to his Waterloo planning. He was a phenomenal administrator and dragged France out of the chaos of the Revolution; the Napoleonic Civil Code of law and civil administration was forced upon subservient nations, but often retained after his demise. His lust for power may have been his greatest strength, but it was also his Achilles' heel. By creating so many enemies, his downfall was inevitable – those who live by the sword are destined to die by the sword.

By the time he faced Wellington at Waterloo, Napoleon was past his best. His father had died of stomach cancer in 1785, and he was beginning to show signs and symptoms himself. He was overweight and physically exhausted, the effort of rebuilding the army and the speed of the campaign must have intensified his illness. These contributed to his muted performance on 18 June 1815. His army however, was full of veterans and vastly superior in experience and ability to Wellington's polyglot force. It was confident of victory, confident in its leader and confident in its invincibility. These traits were to make the consequent series of reverses received at Waterloo harder to bear. Eventually it imploded, becoming nothing more than a terrified rabble.

CHAPTER 3

'LE PLUS BRAVE QUE LES BRAVES'

NAPOLEON described his firebrand of a Marshal who was to effectively lead the French army at Waterloo as 'The Bravest of the brave'. Like Napoleon and Wellington, Michel Ney was born in 1769 but not to nobility but at Saarlouis to a barrel cooper of lowly social status as one of four children. He received what was, for the times, a reasonable education at the hands of monks, and at the age of thirteen embarked upon a career as a notary clerk, a profession he was neither suited to nor enjoyed. Six years later on 6 December 1788, he enlisted as a trooper in a Hussar regiment. Thus began a military career that would end on a cold December morning exactly twenty-seven years to the day after it began.

1789 was to be the year when social status would no longer be the

Ney leads the French cavalry during the massed cavalry assaults at Waterloo. Famous for his courage, Ney had five horses killed under him during the battle but escaped wounding.

principle factor in the achievement of high rank. Ney's rise to the highest military rank in Napoleonic France was due in large part to his legendary bravery and the love of a good fight, the detailed training in a military academy like Napoleon or the ability to purchase command like Wellington were not options for Michel Ney. It still took three years for Ney to get off the first rung of the promotional ladder, but once started, he climbed with alarming speed. By 1792, he had reached the rank of Sergeant Major and later that same year, 20 September, he was to fight his first battle at Valmy, the result of which was a glorious victory to the fledgling Republic of France and further promotion to officer status for Ney as a sub-lieutenant.

A period of serving both as a regimental and staff officer saw Ney promoted to Captain by April 1794 and it was then that he came into contact with General Kléber who was to be his mentor and provide important patronage that would thrust Ney into the limelight of Republican France and eventually to the attention of Napoleon himself. Placed in command of a company of handpicked cavalrymen, Ney was tasked with flank protection, reconnaissance and surgical strikes on the enemy. His courage and tactical sense led to further reward, and by the age of twenty-five, Kléber saw fit to promote his brilliant young leader of partisans to the rank of Chef de Brigade, or Colonel. Not only was Ney displaying his legendary courage, but was showing signs of his real strength, that of unconventional military operations where the individual qualities of the man ranked higher than the number of troops available. Although trained as a conventional soldier, Ney's personality and abilities where more suited to what today would be regarded as Special Forces. Gillet, the local political officer or Representative of the People, commented of Ney: 'men of his stamp are not common'.

In August 1796 at the age of twenty-seven, after capturing the cities of Wuerzburg and Pforzheim, he was made a Brigadier-General. Ney's meteoric rise to senior command was comparable to Napoleon's own martial success, possibly more so as unlike Napoleon, he had risen from the lowest rank in the army structure.

Ney was far from finished with heroic acts and his capture of Mannheim through sheer bluff with only 150 soldiers behind him and his raw courage in the charge not only secured him further promotion but also the adoration of the soldiers throughout the army. Despite his rapidly growing fame, he was still not part of Napoleon's plans or even someone to whom Bonaparte paid a great deal of attention. When Napoleon conducted the Coup de Brumaire in 1799, Ney was unimpressed but agreed to serve and signed the Act of Adherence. Ney became of great interest to Napoleon in 1800 at the Battle of Hohenlinden, when he conducted a bold attack into the centre of the Austrian army, shattering resistance and taking thousands of prisoners. Napoleon recognized a fighter when he saw one, but also recognized a man whom the soldiers adored almost as much as him. It was probably the adoration that drew Napoleon to Ney, possibly recognizing a kindred spirit, he decided that Ney was a man that he needed to reward and keep in closest confidence. Napoleon arranged for Ney to marry a young aristocrat, appointed him Inspector-General of Cavalry and then Ambassador to Switzerland. In 1803 Ney was made a Corps Commander and the day after Napoleon crowned himself Emperor, he created the Marshalate. Ney was elevated to the highest military rank in the land.

In 1808, Ney was despatched to Spain under the command of Marshal Masséna. This came as a shock to Ney who considered himself to be the Marshal of France rather than a Marshal, and thought it beneath him to take orders from any other man than Napoleon. Ney was bettered by Wellington

Marshal Michel Ney in full ceremonial uniform of a Marshal of France (Gerard).

under the command of Masséna at Busaco and led the rearguard during the retreat from Villa-Franca. Unsurprisingly, Ney and Masséna had a turbulent relationship to the extent that Ney's service in the Peninsular was ended in recall to France where he was placed at the head of the 3rd Corps under the direct control of Napoleon.

Ney now embarked upon the campaign that was to be his finest hour, one of the few who would be able to claim any form of enhancement from the trials of the Grande Armée which was to be utterly destroyed in the harsh Russian winter of 1812. After battles at Ostrovno, Smolensk and Borodino, the French Army reached Moscow, only to find that the Russians had set the city ablaze and destroyed or removed all the food stocks. The Retreat from Moscow then began as the winter turned and Ney

Ney, one of the few who returned from Russia in 1812 with his reputation enhanced, leads the Rear Guard by example. (Yvon)

Ney rides behind Napoleon and ahead of the other Marshals and Generals. In his own mind, Ney was not a Marshal of France, but rather the Marshal of France. It was an attitude which caused friction throughout his career.

was given command of the Rear Guard. Often to be seen on foot and with a musket in his hands, he led a remarkable resistance, often taking the offensive and preventing the Russians from destroying Napoleon in a pitch battle. Again his personal courage was beyond dispute and as the French finally crossed the Nieman, it was Ney who was 'constantly fighting, retreating but never flying, marching after all the others, supporting to the last moment the honour of Napoleon's arms, and for the hundredth time during the last forty days and forty nights, putting his life and liberty in jeopardy just to save a few more Frenchmen'. Napoleon, probably stunned by the fact Ney was still alive, rewarded his indestructible Marshal with the title 'Prince de la Moskowa'.

Staying close to Napoleon, he fought in all the major engagements of his Emperor in the next two years, but the defeat at Leipzig by the combined armies of Russia, Austria and Prussia made him reappraise his loyalty, choosing France ahead of Napoleon. At Fontainbleau, Ney was amongst those Marshals who requested, and received, the abdication of Napoleon and then carried the abdication papers to the Tsar of Russia.

With Napoleon in exile, Ney swore allegiance to the restored Bourbon monarchy and was allowed to keep all his titles as well as being placed in command of the Royal Guard. The Bourbon court was not a place for a cooper's son, and soon Ney was finding that his lowly roots were the source of much courtly amusement. When his wife was insulted by the Duchesse d'Angoulême, Ney's temper exploded, he barged past the Guards with the line 'out of my way, lackeys' and proceeded to tear a strip off the arrogant Duchess and threw in what he thought of the Bourbon dynasty for good measure. Ney then retired to his estates, his outburst having thrilled the majority of the French population and helped set the scene for Napoleon's return.

Despite his extraordinary success, Ney was no great tactician and even less a strategist. His approach to command was to lead from the front, inspiring men to great actions through his own immense personal courage. Napoleon recognized this and for all his experience and status, Napoleon was disinclined to give Ney his own command. At Ulm and Jena, Eylau and Friedland, Ney served under Napoleon, leading his corps like some huge formation of storm troopers, always at the critical point and basking in the reflective glory of the Emperor and the title Duc d'Elchingen.

In essence, Ney was a simple soldier who was a leader of men in battle rather than a leader of a strategic campaign. His own honour was paramount to him, refusing promotion on more than one occasion as he felt his own actions were unworthy of reward. His primary loyalty was to France, not Napoleon or the Bourbons. He was cursed with a fiery temper that smouldered on a very short fuse and this above all clouded his vision. His temperament was matched by his appearance; his shock of red hair and stern appearance and battlefield aggression led to a variety of nicknames including 'Michel the Red' and 'The Red Lion.' Napoleon was heard to say when Ney caught up with him on 15 June 1815 that 'all will be well, Old Red is here'. He was, in what polite society would describe, as 'rough around the edges' and was acutely aware of his humble beginnings but felt he deserved every honour and title that had been showered upon him. Ney was, apart from being ridiculously brave, exceptionally tough and took hardship in his stride. After Lutzen, in 1813, he appeared in front of Napoleon straight from the battlefield who expressed concern about the vast quantity of blood that covered his Marshal. Ney calmly retorted 'it isn't mine, Sire, except where that bullet passed through my leg'. Lutzen was not the only battle in which Ney was wounded; the long list also included Leipzig and Smolensk where he received a musket ball in the neck.

Ney was fortunate to have any part in the Waterloo campaign after Napoleon found out that he had promised the King to bring the escaped Emperor back to Paris 'in an iron cage'. But forgiven he was and caught up with Napoleon on 15 June and immediately given command of a wing of the army. The fact that the wing was spread over fifteen miles and Ney was unsure of who was commanding what divisions was hardly his fault. However, the disposition of his troops and his own limited knowledge of the commanders severely disadvantaged him on 16 June when he took to the field opposite Wellington at Quatre Bras.

PART TWO
Prelude to Battle
20 April 1814 – 17 June 1815

Soldiers! In my exile, I heard your voice...Put up your tricolore cockade! You wore it in our greatest battles...Do you think this handful of arrogant Frenchmen can stand the sight of them...They are the enemies...Victory will advance at the charge.

NAPOLEON, March 1815

Soldiers, that man Bonaparte, who recently in the face of all Europe abdicated a usurped Power of which he made so fatal a use, has now landed once more on French soil, which he ought never to have seen again.

MARSHAL SOULT, March 1815

CHAPTER 4

'THE COMMON ENEMY TO THE PEACE OF THE WORLD'
(THE POLITICAL SITUATION IN 1815)

The Duke of Wellington in his letter to Lord Beresford after the Battle of Waterloo stated that 'Napoleon did not manoeuvre at all. He just moved forward in the old style, and was driven off in the old style...I never saw the British infantry behave so well'. To draw an analogy with the Wild West, Wellington's army, the beleaguered pioneers, adopted a defensive posture, grimly holding on and waiting for the cavalry to arrive in the form of Field Marshal Gebhard von Blücher's Prussians. Napoleon Bonaparte's army, the Indians, hurled themselves forward in ever increasingly wild attacks, often suicidal, in order to win the day before the cavalry could influence events. As with any analogy, it is not strictly accurate, but in essence is broadly correct. Wellington's plan was to let Napoleon dictate events and counter them as required until Blücher arrived. Conversely, Napoleon's plan was to defeat Wellington quickly before dealing with the Prussian threat. Other analogies have been drawn with Waterloo, one of the most frequent being of two prize-fighters, too exhausted to do anything other than stand toe-to-toe exchanging ever increasingly tired punches. Whatever analogy you prefer, the fact remains that 18 June 1815 was one of the bloodiest days in history. In the space of nine hours, 50,000 men became casualties at rate of nearly 100 per minute, many by either being ordered forward against all military logic of the age or standing firm in the face of an onslaught. Waterloo is a story not only of carnage on a huge scale, but of immense courage and loyalty shown by men who were living a nightmarish hell of noise, smoke, pain, blood, fear and confusion.

To fully comprehend why the respective commanders acted the way they did on 18 June 1815, one must understand the political situation that led up to the battle. Although Wellington and Blücher trusted each other, the same could not be said of General Augustus von Gneisenau, the powerful Prussian Chief of Staff, who openly distrusted Wellington and the British. Had the wound he sustained at Ligny incapacitated Blücher, it is possible that Gneisenau would not have appeared at Waterloo, instead withdrawing his army to Liège. Napoleon may have, at his most politically secure, retired from the field mid-afternoon and sought to re-engage at a later date after General Drouet d'Erlon's attack failed and General Honoré Reille's Corps embroiled itself in the battle for Hougoumont. Napoleon could not trust the political manoeuvrings of the supporters of the deposed Bourbon dynasty in Paris and could not afford a single failure in June 1815. Consequently, he did not withdraw and Waterloo became a decisive battle.

In April 1814, the combination of powerful European Allied forces and internal Royalist treachery led by Charles Maurice de Talleyrand, forced Napoleon to abdicate. Despite fighting a magnificent defensive campaign, Napoleon was betrayed by both politicians and his own generals who were concerned about their future positions once the Bourbon's had been restored in Paris. The Emperor was sent to exile on Elba, a small

Charles Maurice de Talleyrand, diplomat and survivor. Talleyrand's loyalties were purely to himself and was one of two men Napoleon stated he should have hanged if he was to hold on to power.

Mediterranean island with 1,000 men as a bodyguard. As he departed to begin his exile on 20 April 1814, no one could possibly have envisaged what the greatest general of his age would achieve with such a small force less than a year later.

Before Napoleon was sent to exile, the Allies had not been united; they shared different aims and were, in general, financed by the British Government. Prominent in all the political chicanery was Lord Castlereagh, the British Foreign Secretary. Throughout the period, Castlereagh often hid the true extent of the terms and conditions of deals he had made from his own government and entered into numerous private agreements with individual Allies that the British as a nation would be expected to keep. At the Treaty of Vienna, designed to carve up the French Empire, the Alliance began to disintegrate. The meddlesome Castlereagh, who appeared to be following his own policy rather than that envisaged by his government, compounded diametrically opposed aims and ambitions. Meanwhile other individual Allies began to follow Castlereagh's lead, and various national representatives made a series of conflicting secret deals. Because of this, mistrust developed at an unhealthy rate between all the Allies, but particularly against Britain. At one stage, it appeared that war between the Allies was inevitable.

Lord Castlereagh led the political chichanery that took place during the period of peace when Napoleon was on Elba.

France had been changed irreversibly by the 1789 Revolution. As the nobility returned from their own exile they found that the peasants were no longer afraid of them, and the Catholic Church could no longer weald the same power as it had in its halcyon years. The restored Bourbon, King Louis XVIII, conducted himself as if nothing had changed for the past twenty-five years. He still believed firmly in the absolute power of the Divine Right of Kings and many of the ordinary citizens of France began to feel that the Revolution was defeated; all the advances it had made towards democracy were being destroyed. Louis XVIII failed to comprehend the delicate and precarious nature of his position. If he were to survive in place, he would require the absolute loyalty of the army. It was an army that loved Napoleon for all the glory he had given it, for sharing its discomforts and for knowing his business as a soldier. The Bourbons made the army suffer not just from poor pay and uniforms, inadequate accommodation and rations, but also by the new corps of royalist officers, many of whom were inexperienced dandies. Napoleon's marshals were generally treated poorly and although allowed to keep their rank and titles, they were belittled whenever possible. Only Marshal Nicholas Soult did well, becoming the Bourbon Minister for War and making him thoroughly disliked throughout the army.

An incident involving Marshal Michel Ney, the 'bravest of the brave', was to bring the resentment felt throughout France to the surface. After one insult too far, Ney launched a personal verbal assault directly at the Royal family, news of which spread like wildfire throughout the country. France resented the Bourbon restoration and a second revolution seemed to be close to coming, all it required was a catalyst and that came in the form of Napoleon. On 1 March 1815 he landed in the south of France, complete with his less than awe-inspiring force of 1,000 men. The troops sent to defeat him flocked to Napoleon and on

Louis XVIII did more than anyone to generate the atmosphere for the triumphant return of Napoleon by refusing to accept or embrace change.

8 March, he captured Grenoble, and doubled his original force. Napoleon marched northwards, his 'army' growing daily and on 10 March, he captured Lyon and his ranks swelled to 18,000. The following day, the main hope for the Bourbons, the less than enthusiastic and sorely tested Ney, declared for Napoleon stating that he was the 'legitimate dynasty

chosen by France.' Soult remained loyal to Louis XVIII, but even he would eventually desert the sinking Bourbon ship. On 19 March, Napoleon was in Auxerre, only a one-day march from Fontainebleau, forcing a terrified Louis XVIII to flee Paris at midnight. On 20 March, Napoleon entered Paris, in less than three weeks he had captured France, without a shot being fired or a casualty sustained. More importantly, the vast majority of the population was supportive of him.

Napoleon immediately initiated the rearming and reforming of the Army, putting the entire national effort behind the production of weapons and equipment. At the same time as he was rapidly rebuilding his fighting machine, he wrote to all his European enemies requesting peace and giving up various claims to territory. Without exception, the Allies refused him and urgently began formulating plans to destroy Napoleon. To stay in Paris and wait for his enemies to muster would invite disaster; Napoleon had no choice left open to him but to go on the offensive. Many royalist ministers remained in positions of authority, most notably Talleyrand, but Napoleon did not have the time available to him to neutralize these potential problem-makers. He simply could not afford to fail. Napoleon realized that he would need to fight a swift and successful campaign before he could turn his attention towards securing his political base and the future Bonaparte dynastic succession.

The return from Elba was meant to have been halted by the 5th and 7th Line Regiments, but the troops flocked to Napoleon. (Steben)

CHAPTER 5

'I CAUSED THE MISFORTUNES OF FRANCE, I OUGHT TO REPAIR THEM'

(PLANS OF CAMPAIGN AND THE ADVANCE TO CONTACT)

NAPOLEON'S PLAN was audacious, simple in its conception yet required detailed planning and initiative of the highest order by the officers who would execute it. In essence, he intended to keep the Allies separated and defeat each in turn. The Allied plan was diametrically opposed, again simple in concept but required great trust between nations, something that was sorely lacking in early 1815. The armies of Britain, Netherlands, Prussia, Russia and Austria would fight a combined campaign and overwhelm Napoleon's numerically inferior forces.

Amongst Napoleon's enemies, there was deep-rooted mistrust, a situation that the Emperor planned to exploit. The Tsar of Russia made no secret of his dislike of the Bourbon family and knew he would receive Poland from Napoleon if the latter offered peace. Although the Tsar stated that a Russian Army numbering 200,000 would advance westward to face

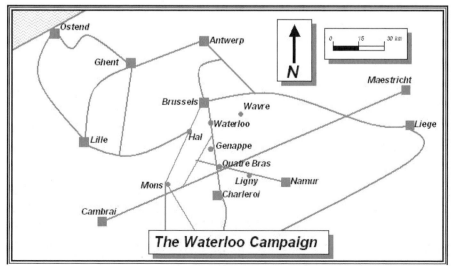

The Waterloo Campaign

Napoleon, he did not intend to complete this manoeuvre with alacrity. It was probable that the Tsar intended to see how Napoleon fared against the other Allies before he decided on his real course of action. Austria was on the verge of war with Prussia and Russia and could not afford to lose men fighting Napoleon and then face further conflict. The British Army had either disbanded or sent most of the Peninsular War veterans to the Americas, leaving a small army with few experienced soldiers. The Netherlands had recently gained its independence and would be fierce in the protection of that status, but many citizens, particularly those in the area that today is Belgium, had fought for Napoleon and were not adverse to him. Prussia was itching to seek revenge for the humiliations heaped upon it by Napoleon but was facing the possibility of war with Austria and had little trust for Britain, especially since the revelation of a secret treaty between Bourbon France, Britain and Austria against Prussia and Russia.

The British once again were prepared to finance the struggle against Napoleon and two armies began to form in Belgium. The Prussians under Blücher totalled some 116,000 men and a combined Anglo-Dutch army, known as the Allied Army, under the field command of Wellington but with complex national restrictions, totalled 88,000. Also in the Allied Army were units from Hanover (not to be confused with the King's German Legion, who although Hanoverian, were British units), Belgians, Brunswickers and Nassauers. Apart from the complexities of the national command restrictions, language differences further compounded the smooth running of Wellington's force. The Prussians and Allied Army converged on Belgium with the intention of combining and fighting together, but with other independent contingency plans should things go wrong. Blücher would be interested in safeguarding his line of communication through Liège whilst Wellington was fully aware of the importance of Ostend to Britain as its port of entry to Europe. From Brussels, these two locations would split the forces facing Napoleon and make it easier for him to defeat the two armies separately.

Napoleon's situation was completely different. When he began crossing the French border in the early hours of 15 June, he had an army of 123,000 in the field. A further 400,000 troops were posted in France and more were being recruited daily. He was of the opinion that if threatened, both Blücher and Wellington would fall back on their respective lines of communication and therefore aimed to drive a wedge between them at the place where the two armies met, Charleroi, which he secured by the

Field Marshal Blücher, commander of the Prussian Army harboured an immense personal hatred for Napoleon.

Emmanuel Grouchy was created a Marshal at the start of the campaign. Although a respected cavalry commander, he had no experience in All Arms Groupings.

evening of 15 June. Napoleon had to place enormous trust in his subordinate commanders. At the last minute, he forgave Ney for his 'I will bring him back in an iron cage' remark made to royalists when tasked with capturing Napoleon on the latter's advance on Paris from exile. Ney was given command of the left wing of the army, but was only appointed and briefed as to the plan after he had reached Napoleon in the afternoon of 15 June. Consequently, Ney was forced to plan on the move with his troops spread out between the frontier and Charleroi, and was therefore disadvantaged from the onset. Marshal Emmanuel Grouchy commanded the right wing of Napoleon's force, he was a talented cavalry commander but inexperienced at handling all-arms groupings. Marshal Soult became Napoleon's Chief of Staff; a remarkable appointment considering the level of loyalty he had shown to the Bourbons. Soult was a brilliant planner, but lacked the experience of communicating Napoleon's thoughts to orders and therefore was left wanting in his ability to execute.

Much has been made of Wellington's attendance at the ball hosted by the Duchess of Richmond on the night of 15/16 June. In truth, it acted as a focal point for all of Wellington's senior commanders for briefing and installed an air of calm in the Belgian capital. Wellington had in fact made a potentially serious miscalculation in that he had ordered his forces to concentrate at Nivelles, creating a thirteen mile gap between himself and Blücher. What Wellington was not to know until later was that Napoleon was in fact ten miles beyond Charleroi and Ney was using the road that split the gap between himself and Blücher as his axis of advance. Fortunately for Wellington, two officers of the Netherlands army, General Jean-Victor Rebeque and General Hendrik-George Perponcher had realized the danger and, against orders, stationed themselves at the crossroads of Quatre Bras.

Napoleon's plan for 16 June was to inflict a crushing defeat on the Prussians who he thought would muster no more than 40,000 in time to meet him. If Ney could secure the strategically important crossroads of Quatre Bras, it would prevent Wellington from supporting Blücher and allow Ney to hammer into the flank of the Prussians, ensuring a decisive victory. For reasons known only unto himself, Napoleon did not issue orders overnight of the 15/16 June, instead waiting until 7.00 am. This delay gave both Wellington and Blücher time in which to correct their errors and prepare to face the French.

At Ligny, Blücher managed to field some 80,000 men, twice the figure estimated by Napoleon and presented the Emperor with a conundrum. This was too large an army to crush with the numbers Napoleon had available, and he required more men from Ney's force. He consequently dispatched a Staff Officer to redirect d'Erlon's Corps from Quatre Bras to Ligny. What transpired from that fateful errand was one of the underlying reasons for failure in Napoleon's strategy.

Ligny was a battle of attrition that did not get underway until 3.30 pm. The Prussians lost approximately 12,000 men and Blücher himself was injured. Gneisenau assumed command of the Prussian army and by nightfall was forced to withdraw. Gneisenau's instinct was to withdraw towards Liège, but the plan of campaign was to stay in contact with

Marshal Soult, Napoleon's Chief of Staff at Waterloo

Wellington acknowledges the salutes from troops during the withdrawal from Quatre Bras.

Wellington. Wellington had promised to come to the aid of the Prussians at Ligny 'if I am not attacked myself.' Gneisenau had understood that to mean a definite presence of British troops and was therefore even more mistrustful of Wellington when this did not transpire. He then made a decision that Wellington would describe later as 'the decisive moment of the century,' Gneisenau compromised between Liège and Wellington and ordered a withdrawal to Wavre, 18 miles north of Ligny.

At Quatre Bras, Wellington had some 6,500 troops belonging to Rebeque and Perponcher in position at daybreak. The remainder of the army had been ordered to Quatre Bras and was spread out between there and Nivelles. It was a highly precarious situation for Wellington, but he

was again helped by a lack of French urgency.

At 8.00 am. Ney received orders from Soult to 'occupy Quatre Bras and be prepared to advance to Brussels.' There was no hint of urgency and no time scale in which he should operate. Ney's first units where ready to advance at 11.00 am. when he received a second message from Soult, informing him that Quatre Bras was strongly held and he was to keep his two Corps (Reille's and d'Erlon's) and his cavalry closed up. Ney's troops were spread across fifteen miles and so he halted and waited for d'Erlon to close with him. On reflection, Ney estimated that d'Erlon would take the remainder of the day to do this and he decided to move forward again but with caution.

When he reached Quatre Bras, the lay of the land made estimation of enemy troop strengths extremely difficult. The caution that had been encouraged through his orders and the experience of Reille in fighting Wellington, allowed a further two hours for Wellington to get troops into the area. When the attacks eventually began, the lead elements of the Allied Army were nearby. As the courageous men of Rebeque and Perponcher's force began to fail, General Jean-Baptiste Van Merlen's Dutch cavalry arrived shortly followed by General Sir Thomas Picton's British infantry division.

As d'Erlon was in sight of Quatre Bras, where his presence would still have been decisive, Napoleon's Staff Officer reached him with orders to march to Ligny. D'Erlon faced east and began to hurry to his Emperor, but neither he nor the Staff Officer chose to inform Ney of the situation. When Ney discovered half of his infantry was heading in the wrong direction, he sent another Staff Officer after them to redirect them onto Quatre Bras. As d'Erlon came in sight of Ligny, where again his presence would have been decisive, he turned around and marched back to Quatre Bras. D'Erlon therefore did not grace either engagement with his presence and this allowed both the Prussians to withdraw intact and Wellington to hold the strategic crossroads.

Napoleon's plan to destroy the Prussians had failed, although his enemies were prevented from linking up. As long as that remained the case, Napoleon could still defeat Wellington and Blücher in detail. On the evening of 16 June, Napoleon decided to take a risk; he sent Grouchy with a third of the army after the Prussians. Grouchy's task was to prevent the Prussians joining Wellington, therefore allowing Napoleon to focus his attention on the Allied Army. Grouchy's subsequent failure to prevent the bulk of the Prussian Army reaching Waterloo on the evening of 18 June ensured that Napoleon's defeat was total.

PART THREE
An Outline of the Battle
18 June 1815

The history of a battle is not unlike the history of a Ball. Some individuals may recollect all the little events of which the great result in the battle won or lost; but no individual can recollect the order in which, or the exact moment at which, they occurred which makes all the difference as to their value or importance.

DUKE OF WELLINGTON, August 1815

Winning a battle has never been about killing the enemy, but about generating and maintaining a level of violence that it breaks his 'will to resist.'

LIEUTENANT-COLONEL CHRIS KEEBLE PARA
School of Infantry, Warminster, 1985

CHAPTER 6

I HAVE JUST RIDDEN ALONG THE WHOLE LINE, AND I NEVER SAW A WORSE POSITION' (DAWN - 11.30 AM)

JUST BEFORE DAWN on the morning of 18 June, Wellington received confirmation from Blücher that he intended to march to the Duke's aid with at least one Corps. This was the information he needed and at that point committed his army to battle.

Three building complexes anchored Wellington's position. On his right and forward of the main position, effectively dominating no-mans land and preventing a flanking envelopment, was Hougoumont. During the night, men of the Grenadier, Coldstream and Scots Guards had occupied and prepared Hougoumont and the surrounding area for defence. Located a few hundred yards forward of the crossroads in the centre of Wellington's position was the farm complex of La Haie-Sainte, occupied by Major George Baring of the King's German Legion. On the left of Wellington's position was the Papelotte farm complex protected by the Nassau troops of the Prince of Saxe-Weimar. In addition, the river Smohain and the boggy ground on the left of the line made a flanking envelopment by Napoleon exceptionally difficult. Along the ridge, Wellington deployed his army, skilfully placing untried units between reliable troops in order to give moral support and example. The troops were located on the reverse of the ridge in order to protect them from artillery but also to hide from Napoleon the true extent of his dispositions. Content with his arrangements, Wellington turned to the Spanish Ambassador to the Netherlands and commented 'the French are going to get the devil of a surprise when they see how I defend a position.'

When Napoleon saw the Allies still occupying the ridge, he was confident of an easy victory. 'There is no longer time for them to retreat' he observed, 'Wellington has gambled and lost. He has made defeat certain.' His good mood was evident as he took breakfast with his senior officers, announcing that dinner would be taken in Brussels that evening and even ordered mutton for the occasion. Napoleon's retort to Soult's doubts as to the expected ease of the forthcoming victory displayed utter confidence

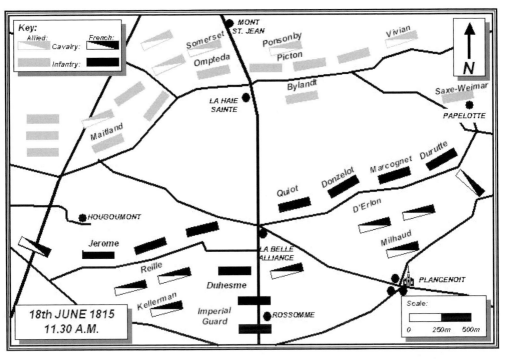

that bordered on contempt for his opponents: 'Just because Wellington has defeated you, you think he is a great general. I tell you Wellington is a bad general, that the English are bad troops and that this is going to be a picnic.'

Napoleon decided to delay the start of the battle; the official reason given was that the extra time should be allowed for the ground to dry a little. A few hours would have made little difference to the ground, but would have allowed time for the rest of his army to get into position, find and eat its breakfast and most importantly, to dry and prepare its weapons. To Wellington, any delay by Napoleon was manna, for every hour of delay meant the Prussians would be closer to him when the battle eventually started. It appeared that the French had not learnt the lessons of Ligny and Quatre Bras.

At approximately 9.00 am Napoleon gave his last briefing, his outline plan was simple in the extreme and ultimately was followed to the letter. 'I shall bombard them with the great weight of my artillery, I shall charge them with my cavalry, so that they show themselves and, when I am quite

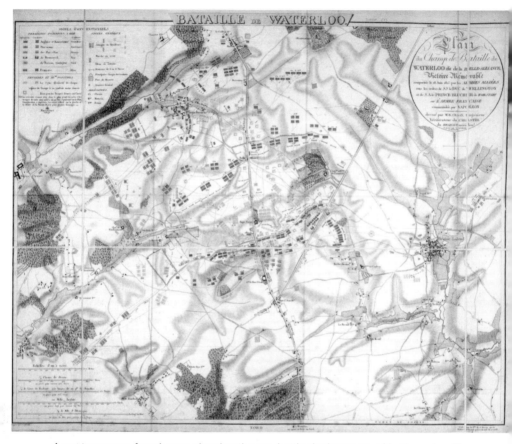

A contemporary french map showing the pre-battle deployments of both armies. The map is upside down with the northern edge at the bottom.

sure where the English troops are, I shall march straight at them with my Guard.' Napoleon planned a diversionary assault on Hougoumont in order for Wellington to weaken his centre by reinforcing his right, then launch d'Erlon's Corps on the eastern end of the valley, turn into the centre and roll up the Allied position. The French troops were formed west to east along a ridge of which La Belle Alliance marked the centre, and it was here that Napoleon spent much of the morning reviewing his soldiers before retiring to the farmhouse at Rossomme, leaving Ney in control of events.

CHAPTER 7

'THERE IT GOES'
(11.30 AM - 3.00 PM)

BATTLE was joined at approximately 11.30 am when Prince Jerome, Napoleon's brother, launched the first of the attacks against the farm-château Hougoumont. The initial assault lasted 30 minutes as the outlying defenders withdrew through the wood towards the buildings where the attack was defeated. This failure appeared to enrage Jerome who proceeded to throw more and more men forward in a desperate attempt to capture the buildings.

As the attacks on Hougoumont were taking place, Napoleon began to assemble the 'Grand Battery' of approximately 80 guns running from La Belle Alliance along the ridge to the right of his position. These guns were to bombard the Allied troops and provide supporting fire to d'Erlon's Corps as it delivered a hammer blow to the Allied line, splitting it into two. It was to then turn into the centre and destroy the Allies with an irresistible

The opening move of the battle was directed at Hougoumont, the location chosen by Wellington to secure his right flank.

wave. This daring move, if successful, would ensure the rapid defeat of Wellington's polyglot army and free Napoleon to focus entirely on the Prussians. At approximately 1.00 pm, the Grand Battery opened fire. Simultaneously, Napoleon received the first reports of Prussian activity to his extreme right, emphasising the importance of a rapid success by d'Erlon. Between 1.30 pm and 1.45 pm, d'Erlon's 16,000 strong Corps descended the ridge and advanced across the valley separating the two armies, dividing itself into three components as it advanced. The left hand division under General Quiot attacked La Haie-Sainte, and the right hand division under General Pierre Durutte stormed into the farm complexes of Papelotte, Smohain and La Haye. The remaining two divisions under General Pierre-Louis Marcognet and General François Donzelot drove straight towards the Allied line on a collision course with British and Belgium troops under Picton.

Drouet, Comte d'Erlon, failed to appear either at Quatre Bras or Ligny and his Corps was comprehensively smashed in the early stages of Waterloo.

General Bylandt's Belgium brigade, which had fought so bravely at Quatre Bras, was in a forward slope position throughout the bombardment and had suffered horrendous casualties. As the full might of d'Erlon's Corps descended upon them, it is of little surprise that the Belgians broke and ran back through the British troops positioned on the reverse slope. Picton, outnumbered three to one, immediately ordered his Division forward to meet d'Erlon. The Gordon Highlanders received a devastating volley and wavered, but still Picton's troops came forward, fired and then charged with the bayonet. D'Erlon's Corps was checked by the ferocity of the British counter-attack, but by sheer weight of numbers it was bound to prevail; momentarily, both Napoleon and d'Erlon must have been confident that success was imminent. Whether Picton was confident of holding the attack we will never know, he was struck by a bullet to his temple and was killed.

What followed was probably the defining moment of the battle. The

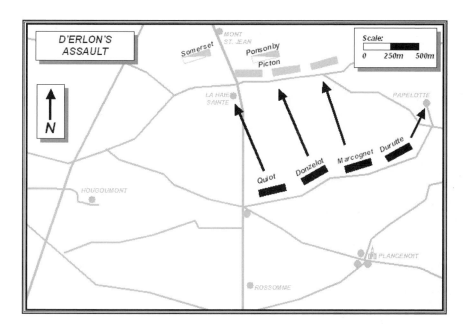

The death of Sir Thomas Picton at the head of his Division in the defeat of d'Erlon's assault.

Earl of Uxbridge, the Allied cavalry commander and Wellington's deputy, had been watching events unfold from the other side of the Allied position and realized the full implications if d'Erlon broke through. He galloped across to the British heavy cavalry and on his own initiative ordered them to charge d'Erlon's assault. The effect upon the French was utterly devastating. Unformed infantry were at the mercy of the cavalry who literally cut their way through the panicking Frenchmen. All control and cohesion was lost as d'Erlon's Corps went from the cusp of victory to chaotic remnants in the space of a few minutes. The French attack had been broken up and routed with huge casualties. It would take much precious time to reform the Corps into an effective fighting unit. The Union Brigade under General Sir William Ponsonby continued its charge through the French and in turn lost its cohesion. Ad hoc groups made it as far as the Grand Battery where they sabred the gunners. These groups on spent horses where easy prey for the French lancers to the extent that by the time they were rescued by the light cavalry of General Sir Hussey Vivian's brigade, they were reduced to less than 50 per cent of their original strength. Ponsonby was amongst the dead. The Union Brigade had undoubtedly saved the day, but the cost meant Wellington had lost much of his offensive heavy cavalry capability. To the right of d'Erlon's assault, Durutte had met with success, temporarily securing Papelotte and part of the hamlet of Smohain. However, the boggy ground and the increasing Prussian threat ensured that a flanking operation launched from this gain would be impractical.

The Earl of Uxbridge, commander of the Allied cavalry and deputy to Wellington. He was responsible for the charge that smashed d'Erlon's attack and was to loose his leg in the closing stages of the battle. (JA Atkinson)

If Wellington had lost his heavy cavalry capability, then Napoleon was left in a position that was far more precarious. More and more troops from Reille's Corps were being sucked into the supposed diversionary attack at Hougoumont that had developed into a battle within a battle. Grouchy was away with a third of his army and d'Erlon was incapable of offensive action for several hours. Napoleon simply did not have the troops

Sergeant Ewart secures the Eagle of the 45th Line during the Union Brigade's routing of d'Erlon's assault.

available to put together an effective all-arms assault – unless he committed early his beloved Imperial Guard. He was clearly aware of predicament he now found himself in: 'This morning the odds were nine to one in our favour. Now they are six to four.'

With the advantage of hindsight, Uxbridge had played the decisive card during the Battle of Waterloo. It is possible that Wellington did not realize how exposed Napoleon was, and the opportunity was there for him to attack. In latter life he was reported as saying on a number of occasions that if he had been leading his Peninsular War army at Waterloo instead of the mixed grouping he had available, he would have taken an offensive posture and attacked Napoleon. Instead, Wellington chose to stay with his original plan and not risk losing his formation. Time was now on his side, and providing his army did not collapse and could hold on until the Prussians arrived, Napoleon could not win. With both sides either incapable or unwilling to take offensive action, the battle subsided into a period of sustained artillery pressure by Napoleon in order to try to shatter the Allied 'will to resist.'

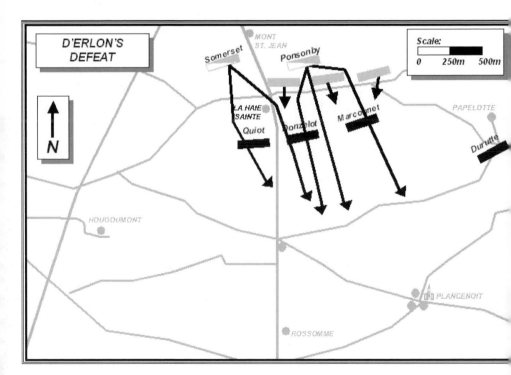

CHAPTER 8

'FORWARD! THE SALVATION OF FRANCE IS AT STAKE.'
(3.00 PM - 6.30 PM)

THE FRENCH artillery was delivering a 'hard pounding' to the Allied infantry causing considerable casualties, but Wellington was aware that artillery alone would not win the day for Napoleon. The danger was that the raw soldiers fighting their first battle might have lost their nerve and fled at the first contact with advancing French. At about 3.00 pm, Wellington ordered the line to withdraw 100 yards in order to find some shelter on the reverse of the slope from the incessant artillery. Ney observed the Allied withdrawal and wrongly assessed that this was a retreat from the field. Desperate not to allow Wellington to escape, he launched General Edouard Milhaud's Cavalry Corps in pursuit in order to

Highlanders in square formation fend off a French cavalry attack. Although the slope up which the cavalry have just charged is exaggerated, the painting clealy shows the intensity of the fighting in the afternoon. (Philippoteauv)

From the Lion Mound it is clear that Ney could not have known that the Allied infantry were unbroken when he launched the mass cavalry attacks. The French approach (A) is clearly uphill towards the Allied artillery along the road (B) leading to Hougoumont and the infantry in squares were located in the dead ground (C) to the rear of the guns. All Allied troops to the north of the ridge adopted by Wellington as his main position were shielded from view, and to a certain degree fire, from the French.

rout the Allies with the words, 'En avant! France depends upon this charge!' Milhaud's Corps had advanced with incredible bravery but ultimately this was a futile attempt to rout the Allies. Once over the ridge, the French cavalry realized that far from withdrawing from the field, the Allied infantry where formed in secure squares, around which they could only trot and slash at with sabres. With no close support artillery to break up the formation, the Allied infantry were receiving their first relief from the incessant bombardment for some hours.

At Hougoumont, all but one division from the entire infantry compliment of Napoleon's left flank had been committed. Reille, the Corps commander had effectively handed over control of his command to Jerome, who had become obsessed with securing the farm complex. It is possible that Napoleon had spoken with his brother and decided that if

Hougoumont fell, Napoleon would switch his line of attack to roll up the Allies from the left. Jerome and Reille had deprived Napoleon of half his infantry and the conversation between the brothers is the only reasonable explanation to account for the behaviour of these officers.

The closing of the North Gate shows the heroic action by Lieutenant Colonel McDonnell and a handful of Guardsmen. Wellington believed that Waterloo hung on the closing of the gate. All Frenchmen who broke into the complex were bayoneted except for a young drummer boy who was made to sit on his drum throughout the rest of the battle.

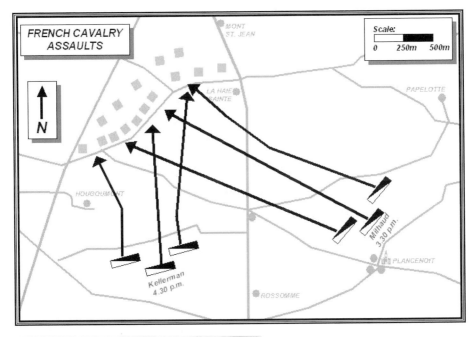

French cavalry encounter the Sunken Road. This painting by Edwards clearly demonstrates the sizable obstacle this presented. Many Frenchmen were simply massacred once they became trapped in the depression.

Napoleon, on returning to the battlefield from Rossomme, observed what Ney had done and far from recalling the cavalry, he launched General François Kellerman's Cavalry Corps to support Milhaud, committing 12,000 cavalrymen to a desperately difficult attempt to dislodge unbroken infantry. The packed ranks of cavalry had to advance uphill, across ground strewn with their dead whilst being shot at with double loaded guns. Once they had closed with the artillery, the cavalry then had to negotiate the sunken road, which broke up what remained of their formation and cohesion. Frustrated by the square formations, the French were repeatedly counter-charged by the Allied cavalry before being forced to withdraw, back the way they came, and suffer even more casualties at the hands of the artillery who remanned the guns. Twelve times they came forward, and twelve times they were repulsed. The French army was bleeding to death against the impassive and disciplined Allied infantry. Wellington knew that the French could not tolerate much more of this punishment 'the battle is mine' he announced, 'and if the Prussians arrive soon, there will be an end to the war.' By 5.30 pm the cavalry had had enough. Exhausted, frustrated and decimated, they withdrew and allowed the artillery to carry on where it had left off a few brief hours previously, inflicting grave punishment upon the Allied infantry.

Ney was desperate for a breakthrough and looked hard to find a crack that could be exploited. The Prussians of General Frederick von Bülow's Corps had been in contact with the Young Guard at Plancenoit and General Hans von Ziethen's troops were beginning to appear in the Smohain area. Gathering what men he could from d'Erlon's Corps

The defence of La Haie Sainte.

(approximately 1,000), Ney succeeded where a whole Corps had failed and captured La Haie-Sainte. Whilst Durutte had met with partial success in the eastern part of the battlefield, the condition of the ground had ensured that this was not exploitable. Ney had secured the farm complex in the centre of the British line astride the Brussels road, and this success was eminently exploitable. The effect of the fall of the farmhouse was devastating on the Hanoverian troops holding the centre of the line and they began break, one cavalry unit fled as far as Brussels where its soldiers proclaimed that the battle was lost. From the stalemate, one audacious move by Ney had given Napoleon a guilt edged opportunity to defeat the Allied Army before the arrival on the battlefield of the Prussians in large numbers.

CHAPTER 9

'HE AND I, AND EVERY OTHER ENGLISHMAN ON THE FIELD MUST STAND AND DIE ON THE SPOT WE OCCUPY.'
(6.30 PM - 8.30 PM)

EVEN whilst Ney was capturing La Haie-Sainte, the Prussians were placing pressure on the French right. Bülow's Corps had captured Plancenoit after a brutal and violent struggle with the Young Guard. Ney dispatched his Aide-de-Camp, Colonel Héymes, to Napoleon with a

The view of the courtyard inside La Haie-Sainte that would have greeted the Frenchmen that stormed through the western gate. The structural interior of the farm complex is unchanged since 1815.

request for more troops to exploit the gap in the Allied centre. Napoleon, clearly preoccupied with the crisis in Plancenoit and possibly unaware of the extent of the opportunity Ney had created gave Héymes a caustic reply to the request, 'Troops? Where do you expect me to find them? Do you think I can make them?' Napoleon then dispatched two battalions of the Old Guard to Plancenoit who drove the Prussians out of the village and 500yds beyond at bayonet point without a shot being fired. Wellington was doing everything in his power to plug the gap in his centre. Units were shunted sideways into the middle of his line, with none more prominent in this action than the Irishmen of the 27th (Inniskilling) Foot. Wellington was later to say that the 27th 'saved the centre of my line', but they did so at a horrendous price, suffering over 65 per cent casualties. Wellington clearly did not intend to withdraw from the field in the face of continual bombardment and the possibility of imminent collapse. To one request for permission to withdraw to cover, he replied, 'He and I, and every other Englishman on the field must stand and die on the spot that we occupy.' With the Prussians nearby, it was vital that the Allies hang on for a little while longer. By 7.30 pm. Wellington had reshuffled his line and the window of opportunity that had existed for an hour, quite literally closed.

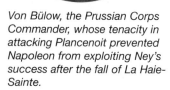

Von Bülow, the Prussian Corps Commander, whose tenacity in attacking Plancenoit prevented Napoleon from exploiting Ney's success after the fall of La Haie-Sainte.

The Allied crisis was past, and it was Napoleon who now stood facing the abyss. Wellington was battered and bleeding, but still astride the Brussels road. Although Plancenoit had been retaken, it was questionable for how much longer the French would be able to resist attempts by Bülow to recapture it. Smohain, the one success in D'Erlon's attack, had fallen to the Prussian's of Ziethen's Corps and it was only a matter of time before it

The Old Guard is offered an honourable surrender. Its refusal resulted in its annihilation.

made its presence felt on the main French line. Napoleon had one last throw of the dice left to him, and he now took that chance. Word was sent down the French line that the blue clad troops of Ziethen's were in fact Grouchy's missing 30,000 men. The French soldiers, believing victory was at last theirs, began to cheer and roused themselves for one final push. At 8.00 pm, Napoleon launched the Imperial Guard, veterans of many battles who had never failed to break its enemy. The French soldiers surmised that the *coup d'grace* was about to be delivered to Wellington's Army, that France was victorious, that Napoleon was still the master of Europe, and all was well.

The Imperial Guard advanced from behind La Belle Alliance, using the

Brussels road as its axis before veering left up the slope now strewn with French cavalry. The path selected put the Imperial Guard on a collision course with the British Foot Guards under General Sir Peregrine Maitland. As the Imperial Guard came over the ridge, the British rose from the rye in front of them and delivered a devastating volley from close range. The Imperial Guard staggered under the impact but began to surge again, only to met by volley after volley of accurate and disciplined fire. The 52nd (Oxfordshire) Light Infantry, under the command of Colonel Sir John Colborne, moved forward and turned to face the flank of the Imperial Guard, pouring enfilade fire into the side of the French formation. It was now too much for the Imperial Guard to take, the withering combination of artillery and musketry was reducing it to a bloody mess and it stopped, staggered and then turned. For the first time, the pride of Napoleon's army had been defeated.

At about the same time as the Imperial Guard was being destroyed by its British counterparts, Ziethen broke onto the battlefield from the woods around Smohain. His line of advance split the French right in two and caused panic to set in. On the other side of the battlefield, the Imperial Guard was in full retreat and the sight of chaos on both sides of the line was overpowering the French soldiers' will to combat. With a growing shout of 'la Garde recule!' the last vestiges of French discipline, morale and resistance collapsed. A route began across the entire line.

CHAPTER 10

'A PRÉSENT C'EST FINI – SAUVONS NOUS.'
(8.30 PM –)

WELLINGTON observed the chaos spreading through the ranks of the French Army and ordered a general advance. The Prussians were appearing on the field in ever increasing numbers and with this, discipline was shattered within Napoleon's army. As the exhausted Allied troops advanced, only the remnants of the Imperial Guard were offering any real resistance. Retreating in a square formation, stopping to beat off cavalry attacks, the Guard was overtaken, just to the south of La Belle Alliance, and the end for these brave soldiers was on hand. Asked to surrender with honour, the reply was explicit in its simplicity, 'Merde!' The Guard was raked by grapeshot and musketry from close range and died *en-masse*, still in formation. Napoleon made an abortive attempt to reorganize at Rossomme, but was forced back via Le Caillou to Genappe.

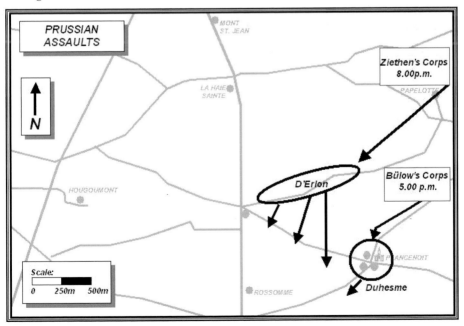

Plancenoit was surrounded and eventually overrun and the Prussians now used cavalry, horse artillery and light infantry to keep an intense pressure on the retreating French. At Genappe, the remnants of the French Army were all trying to cross one bridge and, in the ensuing chaos, Napoleon was nearly captured. The Prussians extracted terrible revenge for the humiliations Napoleon had heaped upon their country. Many Frenchmen were either slaughtered or captured in the Genappe area, and those who did escape were mostly without weapons and held no semblance of order.

Blücher finally met up with Wellington at La Belle Alliance at about 9.00

This rather stylised painting captures the moment Wellington and Blücher met near La Belle Alliance.

Blücher seen at the vanguard of the Prussian pursuit. Wellington's army was plainly too exhausted to continue through the night of 18 June and so it fell on Gneisenau, the Prussian Chief of Staff, to coordinate the brutal and highly effective follow up action. (Dretz)

pm, as darkness began to settle over the battlefield. The two commanders embraced and quickly established the plan for the pursuit. If Waterloo was to be a decisive battle, and there was no reason to suppose that it should not be so, Napoleon must not be allowed to regroup. The Allied Army was clearly in no fit state to conduct pursuit operations and, although the Prussian Army had been marching hard all day, it was in a far less exhausted condition. Gneisenau was instructed to coordinate the pursuit and this was conducted with ruthless efficiency. Throughout the night and the next day, the Prussians snapped at the retreating French heels, ensuring no chance of a rally and that chaos was all the French population would witness as the remnants of the army reached home soil.

Grouchy meanwhile had no idea that Napoleon had been defeated and was still pressuring what he thought to be the main body of the Prussians at Wavre. He was informed of the Emperor's defeat at 10.30 am on 19 June and immediately held council with his generals. It was decided that the wing would not push up to Brussels, as suggested by General Dominique Vandamme, and get behind the Allied armies, but instead withdraw intact to France where he intended to meet up with Napoleon and continue the fight.

Napoleon crossed back into France on 19 June and reached Paris on 21 June. Again, he was defeated by internal political double dealing as much as by his enemies' military action, most notably from Joseph Fouché (who had previously passed Napoleon's Order of Battle to Wellington) and the arch-royalist, Talleyrand. He attempted to escape to the United States, but was betrayed and surrendered to the Royal Navy. He was dispatched to St Helena, a lonely rock in the Atlantic. Here, he spent the rest of his life excusing his own actions, blaming others, (especially the then deceased Ney) and regretting not taking care of internal politics with the same efficiency he usually dealt with military affairs.

CHAPTER 11

'SUCH AN ACTION COULD NOT BE GAINED WITHOUT A GREAT LOSS; AND I AM SORRY TO SAY OURS HAS BEEN IMMENSE'

MUCH GLORY and romance is attached to the story of Waterloo, but the reality makes grim reading; Wellington was deeply affected by the sheer scale of the casualties sustained and prayed that he had fought his last battle. Although the principle commanders escaped physical injury, the immediate staff (Wellington's in particular) and the subordinate commanders themselves were ravaged by the violence of 18 June 1815, most notably the Earl of Uxbridge. Exact figures are not available; most sources agree on a figure of approximately 50,000 men became casualties, but the real figure could be as high as 55,000. Of these, most would have been wounded rather than killed outright at the moment of becoming a casualty. Some would have been mortally wounded and died shortly after being hit, the final outcome being the same even if they had immediately received the very best medical care. For the sake of statistics, these unfortunate men must be counted as those killed outright as a result of the fighting. There were other wounded who would eventually succumb to their wounds, some after a few weeks as in the case of Colonel Sir William De Lancey, Wellington's Chief of Staff, others after several months. It is reasonable to presume that at least two thirds of those who became casualties on 18 June 1815 were wounded, and therefore there would have been in excess of 30,000 men, of all nationalities, requiring treatment following the battle.

Normally the French soldier could look forward to a considerably better evacuation and treatment system than his British counterpart due mainly to the efforts of one man, Baron Jean Dominique Larrey, the father of modern military surgery. Larrey was universally regarded as an honourable man and flourished under Napoleon, becoming the most pre-eminent military surgeon of the age. To the soldiers he was known as 'the soldier's friend' and on more than one occasion had his own horses shot in order that his patients did not go hungry. To Napoleon, he was the man who kept the force levels up by returning many of the wounded quickly to their units. Larrey was left 100,000 Francs in the Emperor's will where he was described as 'the most virtuous man I have ever known'. He was present at sixty battles and was wounded in three of them, including Waterloo, where he was nearly executed by the Prussians who mistook him for Napoleon. His identity was finally established by no less a man than Blücher, whose son's life had been saved by Larrey. Larrey's great contribution, however, was in 'taking the hospital to the wounded' through the use of flying ambulances, thereby revolutionizing the medical procedures from point of wounding. Wounded were transported from Regimental Aid Posts to Divisional Field Hospitals and then through a network of civil contractors to a General Hospital. Larrey introduced *triage* (from the French word 'sort') by which casualties were placed into a priority of treatment. In

Baron Jean Dominique Larrey, 'the soldier's friend' and widely regarded as the father of military surgery. Larrey was fortunate to have survived Waterloo after being mistaken for Napoleon by the Prussians.

contrast to *triage* in a modern civilian hospital where the most serious are treated first, Larrey reversed the principal by treating the least badly wounded as a priority. This ensured that a higher percentage of the wounded survived and had the added military bonus of turning casualties back around onto the battlefield in the quickest possible time.

The British wounded would be, if lucky, given some form of first aid by the Regimental Assistant Surgeon at the point of wounding before having to make their own way back towards more advanced medical assistance. Surgeons treated casualties on a 'first come – first served' basis and

Baron Jean Dominique Larrey developed the triage system and the use of field ambulances. In Napoleon's Egyptian campaign Larrey commandered camels for use as casualty litters, ensuring the French soldier enjoyed the most advanced casualty evacuation system at that time.

therefore many 'minor' wounds would become more serious as a result of the delay in receiving treatment. Although Larrey may be regarded as harsh in his systematic approach, the end result was that many more French survived battlefield wounding. At Waterloo, however, the system failed; initially the sheer weight of numbers overwhelmed the limited ambulances and as the battle was lost, the chaos of the route ensured that the vast majority of the French wounded remained on the field where they fell. For the Frenchman in this unenviable position, an experience worse than the wounding itself had to endured if he was to survive. The victors owned the field and understandably, it was the Allied wounded who were first brought away to the General Hospitals in Brussels. Many Frenchmen suffered two to three days without food and water whilst fighting off death from loss of blood, exposure or looting by Belgian peasants. It must therefore be assumed that a considerable number of Frenchmen who were wounded on 18 June and would ordinarily have survived, died on the battlefield over the next few days. In the case of 27-year old Dominique Modéréact, who was wounded with a musket ball in his brain, was evacuated from the battlefield on the 21 June, lodged in a local village until 30 June before being admitted to the Gendarmerie Hospital and examined on 4 July, finally undergoing surgery on 5 July.

The vast majority of wounds at Waterloo were caused by artillery. High speed projectiles, like grape-shot, would smash bones whilst round shot (cannon-balls) could pass straight through several men, decapitating and ripping limbs off as it went. Treatment for a wound to a joint or any bone injury other than a simple fracture was immediate amputation, with no

Any wound involving a joint or anything more than a simple fracture was immediately amutated. Larrey once conducted 200 amputations in twenty-four hours at Borodino and is seen here about to conduct a double amputation on a wounded French officer.

form of effective anaesthetic and in filthy conditions. As a result, many died from infection, even from the removal of a finger let alone the amputation of a leg from the hip. Military surgeons had to be well versed in the removal of limbs (Larrey once conducted 200 amputations in twenty-four hours at Borodino), and the soldier both remarkably tough and very lucky if he were to survive. Exactly how many amputations were carried out at Waterloo and in the immediate period following the battle is impossible to tell. Two surgeons alone claim to have 680 between them and a further 500 were conducted at Mont St Jean to the rear of the Allied lines. In all probability, the number exceeded 2,500, of whom the majority would have died of gangrene or septicaemia.

If the situation on 18 June was not bad enough, the majority of the 159 Regimental Surgeons and their Assistants departed on 19 June as the Allied Army began its advance into France. The wounded therefore became reliant on the small number of military Staff Surgeons who stayed behind and those still to arrive from England and most importantly upon the skill and care of the local Belgian services and civilian volunteers. One man who made an immediate journey to Brussels on hearing of the battle was Sir Charles Bell, an eminent surgeon based in London.

Sir Charles Bell hurried to Brussels when he heard about the battle, arriving 30 June. Regarded as one of the best surgeons of his era, Bell worked on the Waterloo wounded until his clothes were 'stiff with blood'.

Bell arrived in Brussels on 30 June and immediately began to work on the wounded, operating until his clothes 'were stiff with blood'. Bell was no stranger to the carnage of battle and had made a similar journey to assist British troops at Corunna during the Peninsular War. With Bell and Larrey (despite his having received two sabre cuts and a lance wound) operating and advising others, those who were tough enough and lucky enough to have survived up to that point were now in the best possible hands at that particular moment in time.

Letters written by Staff Surgeons who remained in Brussels for several months after Bell returned to London give updates on the survival or demise of many of the men he operated on. Some are heartbreaking and show the limited understanding of wounding and recovery of the time:

'James Alexander did not survive 48 hours after you saw him...he died, as I have seen many, from the powers of life yielding to an injury they are unable to restore'. Charles Collier, Staff Surgeon

It is also from these letters that we can trace the saga of Dominique Modéréact. His head was opened and musket ball removed by Bell seventeen days after wounding. Modéréact was clearly a highly robust individual whose heartbeat rose a mere eight beats per minute from seventy-two to eighty during the procedure and whose only complaints afterwards were of having a slight headache and a loss of hearing in his right ear. Staff Surgeon Blackadder reports a remarkable recovery that continued until 24 July when Modéréact's pulse suddenly increased to ninety-six beats per minute. Eventually it was discovered that the tough Frenchman had been supplementing his meagre diet with red wine and once access to this self-medication was denied, he resumed his recovery, even regaining some of his hearing. By 6 August, apart from visible 'pulsation of the brain' where part of his skull was removed and skin closed over the weak area, Modéréact had made a full recovery. One can only hope that he went on to enjoy rude health for the rest of his days!

PART FOUR
The Road to Valhalla
(From Waterloo to the Grave)

'When I am dead each one of you will have the sweet consolation of returning to Europe. You will see your relations and your friends; as for me, I shall rejoin my comrades in the Elysian Fields'

NAPOLEON, St Helena

CHAPTER 12

'THANK GOD I HAVE FOUGHT MY LAST BATTLE' (WELLINGTON POST WATERLOO)

WELLINGTON was the conquering hero. The Allied victory at Waterloo brought an end to the Napoleonic struggles and peace throughout Europe. He was showered with gifts, titles, ranks and an enormous quantity of cash. He could have, and perhaps should have, retired to enjoy his considerable wealth and status, but it was neither his style nor his wish.

The carnage and the loss of life at Waterloo clearly had a traumatic effect on Wellington, but the pursuit was on and within a few days the exhausted army that had stood so bravely at Waterloo was advancing into France. Wellington, despite his life of warfare against the French was essentially a Francophile, and the people of France acknowledged that it was Wellington's influence that prevented the worst of the Prussian excesses against them. It was also Wellington who ensured that the peace which followed the final defeat of Napoleon was as generous to the people of France as was possible. Wellington spent the first three years after Waterloo as the commander of the Army of Occupation in France. He was regarded as a fair occupier, his only real blemish being his utter refusal to listen to the appeals of Aglaè Ney as she tried to save her husband's life.

Initially popular, Wellington was known to have had several mistresses, including two who were former mistresses of Napoleon. One of them, Marguerite Josephine Weimer, claimed that he was the more 'vigorous' lover. Although he was clearly a friend to the French people, popularity inevitably turned to dislike and then hatred, and the Duke was lucky to have survived an attempt made on his life. In 1818, he returned to a Britain that was fragile, full of resentment and distrust and financially ruined by the years of warfare that she had financed.

Wellington assumed his place within the Cabinet and despite his appointment being as the Master-General of the Ordnance rapidly became the *de facto* advisor to Castlereagh on foreign affairs. On the death of

Castlereagh, Canning assumed the mantle of Foreign Secretary, but did not share the same relationship with the Duke. Wellington's natural instincts as an archconservative became increasingly apparent: his support for the Corn Laws and his utter refusal to implement or even consider any reform to the corrupt political system of the day. The Duke of York died in January 1827, and the man who had done more than anyone to secure the defeat of successive British armies through epic incompetence (hence the nursery rhyme 'The Grand Old Duke of York') was replaced as Commander-in-Chief by the Duke of Wellington. This appointment was short lived for, in February 1827, George Canning became Prime Minister and Wellington tendered his resignation from the post of Commander-in-Chief and from the Cabinet. For a while, he was sentenced to political wilderness. In August 1827, Canning died and was replaced as Prime Minister by the ineffective Lord Goderich and Wellington again found himself as Commander-in-Chief. But by December 1827, it was obvious that Goderich was not capable of holding high office and with a certain degree of inevitability, Wellington was persuaded by the King to become Prime Minister.

If times were hard and turbulent when Wellington returned to Britain in 1818, they were if anything even harder now. The strength of resentment against the Corn Laws and the demand for political reform, including Catholic emancipation, was immense and even rebellion was a possibility. For a conservative like Wellington, these were difficult times and required every ounce of his limited political and diplomatic skill to avoid the nation slipping into a state of civil unrest. Wellington was acutely aware of the state of public resentment and despite intense opposition from his own party and the King changed his position in order to support the Bill giving Catholics the same political rights as Protestants. Catholic emancipation merely served to open the floodgates for full-scale political reform, and this was a step that the archconservative could not stomach. By today's standards, the situation was ludicrous; Cornwall had only one less seat than all of Scotland, even the ruins of Old Sarum had two seats! Wellington was adamant, in his view the existing system was the best in the world and it possessed 'the full and entire confidence of the country'. For someone who thought so clearly on the battlefield and could see the dire consequences of failure to establish Catholic emancipation, Wellington's unshakable beliefs in a fourteenth century system called into question his political judgement. On 16 November 1830, the Government resigned, thus ending Wellington's life as leader of a nation and not just its army.

Wellington's continual opposition to political reform led him from being the hero of the nation to the most despised man in Britain, regularly being jeered in public. The Reform Bill was passed in 1832, and Wellington was to serve twice more in Government, once as Foreign Secretary for Sir Robert Peel in 1834 and again as Commander-in-Chief in 1841. He retired from active politics in 1846 at the age of seventy-seven, six years before his death, and probably at an opportune time. The Crimean War was looming, and the terrible state of the British Army at the onset of conflict could only be blamed upon the mismanagement of the Whitehall mandarins. Had Wellington not died when he did or had he continued to act as Commander-in-Chief beyond 1846, it would have been highly probable that the blame for much of the privations the soldiers suffered in the Crimea would have been laid at his door.

His last years were quiet, away from the public eye and set in a rigid routine with his time spent either at his country estate of Stratfield Saye or Walmer Castle. He always rose early before attending to his letters until breakfast at 10 am. He was alone again until 2 pm when friends joined him, taking dinner at 7 pm and retiring at 11.30pm. On the morning of 14 September 1852, Wellington chose to stay in bed and summoned a doctor, as he did not feel 'quite well'. During the day he developed breathing difficulties and by 7 p.m. that

Wellington in old age.

evening had died. Queen Victoria wept and to the nation the Iron Duke was once again a hero. He was eighty-three.

The Duke of Wellington was laid to rest beside Nelson at St Paul's Cathedral at the end of a momentous funeral parade. 10,000 troops, representing every regiment in the army and commanded by Major General The Duke of Cambridge formed the core of the procession. No fewer than twelve horses pulled the funeral car and the Duke was carried within four ever larger and more expensive coffins. It was estimated that one and a half million spectators lined the route from Chelsea Hospital to St Paul's, the journey taking four long, slow hours.

In an extraordinary life, Wellington had risen from obscurity to claim the position of the nations leading hero after Waterloo. Although he scaled the political heights in the following years, he was a failure as a politician and nearly lost all his credibility with the nation's populous. Only in death did he once again resurrect his status as the all-conquering hero, a status he was to keep for all history.

CHAPTER 13

'TO LIVE IN CAPTIVITY IS TO DIE A THOUSAND DEATHS' (NAPOLEON POST WATERLOO)

APOLEON was not slow to depart the battlefield of Waterloo. He fled ahead of his shattered army and, apart from narrowly avoiding capture at Genappe by the Prussians, his return to Paris on the 21 June was uneventful. Napoleon had clearly lost the battle, but his mind was still working out his best strategy to continue the fight once the Allies invaded French soil. He knew that Grouchy's force was still intact, he had troops stationed throughout France and the combined forces would give him an army of approximately 250,000. Napoleon firmly believed,

The Imperial Guard desperately hold the ground as Napoleon transfers from the carriage to a horse just outside Genappe. In the chaos of the pursuit Napoleon was nearly captured by the Prussians and it is doubtful if he would have survived summary justice at the hands of Blücher. (Croft)

probably correctly, that he could inflict considerable damage upon his enemies. His hope was that if he could inflict enough damage the Allies would sue for peace and allow him to remain Emperor in a peaceful Europe.

Plainly that scenario was not acceptable to the Allies whose only desired outcome was the total defeat of Napoleon and either his imprisonment or execution. Indeed, if Blücher had captured Napoleon it is doubtful that the latter would have been afforded the luxury of a formal trial. Napoleon committed his final error when he reached Paris. Instead of dissolving the formed Chambers and declaring himself absolute leader of France, he demurred, probably to show he was willing to rule in a democratic France, and once the Chambers had met there was no going back. France was exhausted and thoroughly sick of war. Napoleon abdicated for the second time, now in favour of his son. The Chambers, however, led by Fouché, were immovable. On 24 June, Marshal Davout told Napoleon that he was to leave Paris immediately or suffer arrest. The dream was over, Paris was to be handed over to the Allies without resistance.

Napoleon, a prisoner of the British, on his way to St Helena

Napoleon departed Paris on 29 June and headed for the coast at Rochefort. Clearly he intended to escape from Europe and his chosen destination was undoubtedly the United States. But, to do so, he had to beat the British naval blockade. Having arrived at Rochefort, it was apparent that the blockade could not be broken and so he opted to surrender, with honour, to the British.

On 15 July, Napoleon boarded HMS *Bellerophon*, a captured former French frigate and surrendered to Captain Maitland, stating that he had come 'to throw myself on the protection of your Prince and your laws'. From that day on until his death six years later, Napoleon would remain a prisoner of the British. The *Bellerophon* sailed to Britain, where Napoleon was kept onboard as an object of curiosity, whilst Lord Liverpool's government attempted to find an acceptable solution for the incarceration of their dangerous prisoner. It was decided that Napoleon would spend the rest of his days on the remote island of St Helena. He was transferred to HMS *Northumberland* and arrived at his new home on 27 October 1815.

Napoleon spent the rest of his life as a bitter and depressed individual. He was preoccupied with blaming others for his failings; ran a private campaign against the treatment he received from the British (and especially the much maligned governor, Sir Hudson Lowe); and most importantly, ensuring his own glory would live on long after he was gone.

Napoleon's greatest grievance against the British was that he was treated as a prisoner, not as a guest and was most put out by the use of the title 'General Bonaparte' rather than Emperor. Towards the end, he even accused the British of murdering him by slow poisoning, a statement that would have the conspiracy theorists active until the current day.

Napoleon's most informative notes were undoubtedly his thoughts as to the Waterloo campaign and where it went wrong for him. Unsurprisingly, he accepted no blame for the catastrophe but instead listed a set of 'observations' in which Ney and Grouchy were singled out for particular attention. Of interest was his account of the battle, which bore little or no resemblance to any other contemporary account and was highly critical of Wellington's tactics and ability as a general.

Marshals Ney and Grouchy were not the only men Napoleon chose to blame for his failure. D'Erlon came under attack for his futile counter-march between the battlefields of Quatre Bras and Ligny on 16 June. This is probably the most important factor for Napoleon's failure at Waterloo for if d'Erlon had stayed at Ligny, his arrival would have routed the Prussians and forced Wellington to withdraw upon Brussels. In addition

Longwood House, Napoleon's residence for the last six years of his life.

to these three credible scapegoats, Napoleon also directed blame at General Bourmont for his defection on 14 June thereby weakening the resolve of the troops; General Guyot for launching an unauthorised cavalry attack, and Marshal Mortier for suffering with sciatica and thus depriving him of a competent subordinate commander. Wellington and Blücher were blamed for not conforming to his plans and the weather also received criticism. As for his political demise, Napoleon had an endless list of traitors to blame. Inevitably, and with some justification, he focussed on the manipulative politicians stating 'if I had hanged just two men, Talleyrand and Fouché, I would still be on the throne today'.

Napoleon was ill during the Waterloo campaign and never recovered his health. On St Helena his health gradually declined and the last two years of his life were spent in considerable pain. When the end came, he was delirious, talking of meeting his former comrades and how he would discuss his campaigns with 'Scipio, Hannibal, Caesar, Frederick'. On 5

May 1821, less than six years after Waterloo, 'at the very instant when the cannon was announcing the setting of the sun, his great soul quitted the earth'.

His father had died of stomach cancer before the age of fifty, and Napoleon's great fear was that he would die the same way. The autopsy showed considerable evidence of cancer, particularly through the stomach, but his accusations that the British were trying to murder him was to reach out beyond the grave. Modern research has shown that Napoleon had high levels of arsenic in his body at the time of his death and conspiracy theorists believe that the British were using low level doses to destroy his health. A recent French theory is that a French nobleman, loyal to the Bourbons and with whose wife Napoleon was rumoured to be having an affair, committed the poisoning. More credibly, arsenic was used in small doses as a treatment for certain ailments of the stomach. Napoleon's stomach was unable to break down the arsenic administered for medical reasons, and this would account for high levels found after his death.

Napoleon was buried in a simple grave in Geranium Valley on St

Napoleon died in exile, a bitter and angry individual. (Steuben)

Helena just four days after his death. The British conducted the burial with his coffin borne by troops drawn from the garrison. The coffin was draped with the cloak Napoleon wore at Marengo and his sword. At his graveside, musket volleys were fired and there was a thirty-three gun salute. In 1840, nineteen years after his death, Napoleon was exhumed and the body brought back to France for reburial at Les Invalides. A magnificent tomb was prepared and the funeral procession proceeded down the Champs Elysées, the crowds turned out in their thousands to cheer once more the man who had led Europe to a self-destructive series of wars for his own glorification and endless ambition. Napoleon Bonaparte, Emperor of France, was finally laid to rest.

CHAPTER 14

'THIS IS THE LAST COMMAND I WILL EVER GIVE YOU – FIRE!' (NEY POST WATERLOO)

IF NEY had failed to in his attempt to seek death on the slopes of Mont St Jean, he would find it before the year's end but not in the style of his choosing. The demise of Napoleon's most colourful and energetic Marshal is a savage story of vengeful behaviour, cowardice and tragedy from which only Ney, his loyal wife Aglaé and Marshal Moncey emerge with any credit.

By the time Ney reached France he was probably clinically depressed. He saw no future in resisting the Allies; the army was broken and to continue fighting would cause the further needless loss of life. He realized that he would receive no mercy from the returning Bourbon monarchy and for him the safest possible option was to escape into exile either in Switzerland or more likely America. To this end, he asked for and received two passports from the Minister of Police, Fouché, one in his real name and one with a false identity.

Ney next appeared at the House of Peers where he angrily denounced as a lie the report by the Minister for the Interior, Carnot, that Marshal Grouchy had re-entered France at the head of 60,000 men having defeated the Prussians. He recommended opening dialogue with the Allies. 'I spoke only in the interest of the country' was his reasoning, but the damage had already been done. Ney was now not only an enemy of the Bourbons

Fouché, who provided Ney with two passports, including one with a false name, to aid the Marshal in his escape from France.

but also of the Bonapartists who were already blaming him for the Emperor's defeat at Waterloo. With the nation lined against him it is hardly surprising that Ney was doomed to a traitor's death.

Heading a list of twenty fugitives that the Bourbons intended to suffer the full extent of the law, and at the insistence of his wife, Ney headed south in an attempt to reach Switzerland. He found the roads blocked by Austrian troops and therefore headed to the home of Madame de Bessonis, a relative of Aglaé Ney, near Aurillac. Unfortunately, he was quickly identified. He calmly spoke to his captors who had surrounded the château, asking them whom they sought. 'Come up here and I will show you to him, for I am Marshal Ney'.

While being taken back to Paris Ney was offered the chance to escape.

He castigated the officer concerned, stating that he was a man of honour and 'have given my parole'. Understandably, the Bourbons were concerned about the potential embarrassment that the trial could cause. Even the King exclaimed, 'Why did he allow himself to get caught? We gave him every chance to get away!' But Ney had chosen not to escape and now in custody he knew he must face trial. Ney contemplated 'blowing out my brains' but instead chose to try and clear his name.

It was decided that Ney should be tried by a Court Martial, formed by other Marshals of France. Ney deemed them to be unfit to try him and demanded to be tried by the House of Peers, a move that would maximise publicity and ensure maximum embarrassment for the Bourbons. Only Marshal Moncey refused to take part in the Court Martial of Ney and in an eloquent letter to the King marked his refusal by stating that 'My life, my fortune, all that is dearest to me, belongs to my country and my King; but my honour is my own and no power on earth can wrest it from me; if I am to leave my children my name as their only inheritance, at least it

Marshal Moncey chose to be cashiered and go prison rather than judge the guilt of Marshal Ney.

86

will not be tarnished.' Moncey was immediately cashiered and sent to prison. Of the other Marshals selected, Mortier said he would rather be cashiered but relented, Masséna claimed personal differences would cloud his judgement and Augereau became mysteriously ill and disappeared to bed. The trial started 9 November, with Jourdan replacing the incarcerated Moncey and the others persuaded to sit on the board. They upheld Ney's request for trial in front of the House of Peers, but it was a hollow victory. Augereau stated 'we are all cowards, we should have insisted on a Court Martial to save him from himself.' By going in front of the House of Peers, Ney would be exposed to many more enemies than he would have done in front of his fellow Marshals. Aglaé used the short time she had before the trial sending letters and demanding audiences with the most influential of people. She spoke with the King and also to Wellington, who, to his eternal shame, refused to help seeing the trial purely as an internal French affair and that an example should be made.

Although Ney directed a vigorous and mainly effective defence, the result was a forgone conclusion. On 6 December he was found guilty of treason and sentenced to death by firing squad. The execution was to be carried out within hours of sentencing and set for 9.00 am the following morning (7 December). Ney was informed of the decision at 3.00 am and asked to see his wife and children at 7.00 am. When asked if he wanted a priest with whom he could make his final confession he refused, stating he would 'appear in front of God as I have appeared in front of men. I have no fear.' He was later persuaded to have a senior priest speak with him and who promised to remain with him until the end to administer the last rites. Dressed in civilian clothes, he met with Aglaé and the children for the last time and once they had departed to appeal to the king for a final time, he composed himself for death.

He was not taken to the Plaine de Grenelle where Colonel Labedoyère had been executed as a large crowd was beginning to gather. There were rumours that the veterans would try to affect a rescue and so he was taken to the Place de l'Observatoire where he was stood in front of an end wall. Ney refused to be blindfolded or to kneel, as was the request of the officer commanding the execution stating that 'a soldier does not fear death'. Facing his firing squad, he calmly addressed them:

'I have fought a hundred battles for France and none against her. I protest against my condemnation. Soldiers, this is the last command I will ever give you – fire!'

Of the twelve muskets levelled at him, six balls smashed into his chest, three into his head and one each into his arm and neck. One soldier, unable to shoot his beloved former commander 'had the good sense to fire into the wall above his head.' A Royalist spectator, De Rochechouart was so impressed by the bearing of Ney throughout the ordeal that he turned to his colleague and stated, 'This, my friend, is a great lesson to teach one how to die well.' Ney's body lay on the sodden ground for a full fifteen minutes until the priest had administered the last rites. Many of the spectators celebrated, but one old soldier came forward and dipped his handkerchief into the blood pouring from the shattered body, a final and lasting reminder of the man who had done much to extend the glory of the Empire and had risked all to save French lives.

Ney was buried immediately, given only a plain white headstone with the word 'Ney' engraved upon it. Napoleon, when informed of the execution, initially stated that Ney deserved his fate and although he was to retract this later, he would always hold Ney to blame for his defeat at Waterloo. Although his son would fight to clear his name and Michel Ney would eventually become reconized as one of the heroes of the Napoleonic era, on that miserable December morning, he was not missed by many. When the massive gates of Valhalla opened to allow him entry, there must have been thousands of ordinary Frenchmen who greeted the most colourful of Napoleon's marshals, indeed 'le plus brave que les braves.'

Marshal Ney faced death with his trademark courage, giving 'a great lesson in how to die well'.

PART FIVE
The Footsteps of Command
(The Battlefield Today)

The ground seemed proud to hold so many brave men.

NAPOLEON, St. Helena

CHAPTER 15

'I DO NOT THINK IT WOULD HAVE DONE IF I HAD NOT BEEN THERE.' (WELLINGTON'S WATERLOO)

CONTRARY to popular belief, Wellington did not spend the entire battle, or even the majority of the battle, underneath an elm tree at the crossroads north of La Haie-Sainte. He was to be found at the point of crisis, often redirecting troops himself down to individual battalions. There are numerous memoirs written by men who fought that day reporting sightings of Wellington on or around their positions and therein lies the difficulty of pinpointing Wellington's exact position at any given time. Most of the witnesses would not have been wearing watches and therefore would hazard a guess at the time of their sighting. Those

This contemporary painting of La Haie Sainte from the crossroads in the centre of the Allied line is interesting in that it shows the steep incline that was destroyed by the construction of the Lion Mound.

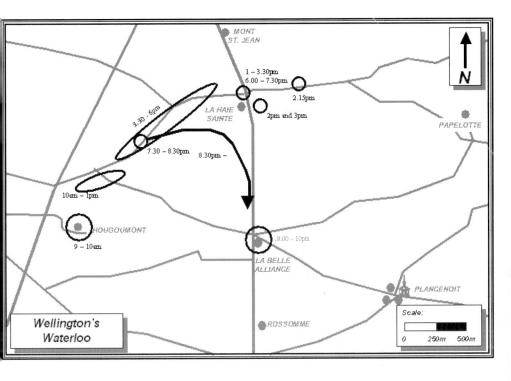

that did have watches did not necessarily record the same time and as a result there is much conflict as to the timings of the Duke's movements, in some cases by several hours. The accompanying map is therefore approximate in its timings, using the most commonly accepted time parameters by witnesses and historians of all nationalities and eras.

Wellington moved continuously throughout the day and generally would have enjoyed a better view of the overall situation than both Napoleon and Ney. This was firstly due to his positioning on higher ground and therefore somewhat above the smoke that would have filled the valley, and secondly because the curved line he adopted due to the Hougoumont salient allowed him lateral vision from west to east across the battlefield rather than a purely north-south view. Napoleon was mainly static throughout the day and spent most of it at either Rossomme or further forward at La Belle Alliance. Ney, who was anything but static, spent most of the battle fighting like the trooper he really was in the smoke filled valley and therefore rarely saw the battle in its entirety. Wellington's

Waterloo village in 1815. The building on the left of the painting served as Wellington's headquarters, whilst the church on the right is the location of many British regimental memorials.

vision of the battle unfolding allowed him to meet each specific French threat with a well-timed counter-measure of his own and was one of the principal reasons for his victory.

Wellington began his day on 18 June when he was woken at 3am at his Headquarters in Waterloo village. He spent the first few hours of the day writing letters before departing the village of Waterloo to rejoin his army on the Mont St-Jean ridge at approximately 7am. After inspecting the line and satisfying himself as to the dispositions adopted, he concentrated his pre-battle efforts on his right (western) flank in the area of Hougoumont. The Duke was particularly concerned that Napoleon might attempt to 'turn' or outflank him west of Hougoumont and therefore the château was crucial to his plans. At approximately 10am he was at the southern edge of the Hougoumont woods, within 300m of Prince Jerome's Division of the

French army, steadying the Nassauer troops in the general vicinity. As he departed, he was shot at by some of the nervous Nassauers, but others put this incident as having taken place on the night of 17 June prior to Wellington departing to his Headquarters in Waterloo village. He returned via the château and inspected the preparations for its defence being made by the Guards under the command of Lieutenant-Colonel McDonnell.

Satisfied that all was well at Hougoumont, Wellington retired to the high ground north and east of the château to observe the preparations being made by his enemy. What he saw from this viewpoint was battle preparations being made by men of Reille's Corps and confirmed that Napoleon did indeed intend to assault on the western side of the battlefield. Wellington decided that he should remain in the area overlooking Hougoumont for at least the opening stages of the battle.

Jerome Bonaparte's Division began the assault against Hougoumont by assaulting through the woods to the south of the château. Wellington

The view of Hougoumont from the main French line and from where the majority of French troops would have advanced from to assault the complex. In 1815 Hougoumont would have been obscured by the woods that were immediately to the south of it.

The view of Hougoumont from the edge of the woods clearly showing the 'killing ground' over which the french had to cross. The plaque on the wall to the right of the picture is to General Bauduin, who led the first French brigade to assault Hougoumont. The gardener's cottage has been added since 1815.

observed the initial French assaults and reinforced the garrison personally, sending forward troops as required. If Napoleon's aim was to make Wellington weaken his centre in order to strengthen the Hougoumont salient, the Duke certainly did not cooperate with him. By locating himself above Hougoumont, Wellington was able to send forward only troops that were really necessary and only from the immediate area, therefore preserving the integrity of the rest of his line. In addition, Wellington had the advantage of lateral vision and by about midday, and certainly no later than 12.30pm, he had noted d'Erlon's preparations taking place on the eastern half of the battlefield. Seeing that a French shell had set the main château ablaze, Wellington sent a message to McDonnell stating that:

'I see that the fire has communicated itself from the Hay Stack to the Roof of the Château. You must however still keep your men in those parts to which the fire

does not reach. Take care that no men are lost by the falling-in of the Roof or Floors. After they have both fallen in, occupy the ruined walls inside of the garden; particularly if it should be possible for the enemy to pass through the Embers in the inside of the house.'

This note, which survives today at the Wellington Museum, Apsley House, shows not only the Dukes attention to detail, but great articulation and coolness under pressure. Satisfied that, the blaze apart, that the French efforts at Hougoumont were being contained, Wellington rode across to deal with the imminent danger posed by d'Erlon's Corps on the other side of the battlefield.

Wellington spent the next 2½ hours of the battle around the crossroads north of La Haie Sainte, but he was by no means static under an elm tree. He was seen at approximately 2pm with the 95th Rifles in the area of the Sandpit and then at 2.15pm on the ridge where his Peninsular War veterans were awaiting the oncoming assault of d'Erlon's infantry. When

The ground over which d'Erlon's Corps had to cover viewed from the position occupied 1st Regiment of Foot (Royal Scots). La Haye Sainte can be seen on the right of the picture.

The Lion Mount now the dominating feature of the battlefield. This extraordinary folly was built as a memorial to the Prince of Orange, but destroyed the sunken road, the key piece of land in Wellington's position.

the two forces collided, Wellington was by his tree, only a couple of hundred meters from the nearest Frenchman. Given his location, it is interesting to note that it was Uxbridge who launched the British heavy cavalry into d'Erlon's Corps. The timing was exquisite and smashed the French formation to pieces, rendering them combat ineffective for several hours and securing the centre and east of the Allied line for the time being. Unlike some historians, Wellington never criticized Uxbridge for ordering the charge, and it is possible that if the latter had not acted on his own initiative then the Duke may well have given the order himself. He was certainly well placed to deliver the blow, had cavalry experience as a regimental officer and would have been fully aware of the devastating impact heavy horses would have on troops mauled by fire and in the process of changing formation. The consequent destruction of the cavalry was due to over excitement and an uncontrollable bloodlust, a common trait in British cavalry troops, and although this would hamper operations later it was not fatal and had bought the Allies several hours of precious time.

What Wellington saw next must have intrigued him. Unbeknown to him, Napoleon was resting away from the battlefield at Rossomme and Ney was now in effective command of the French Army. The Duke would now have seen the French heavy cavalry preparing to attack and although the sight was certainly impressive and possibly even chilling, it meant some relief from the incessant artillery bombardment. What the Duke would also have noticed was that the attack was to be made by cavalry alone, he therefore moved back along the ridge to the area where the Lion Mound is today and began organising his infantry to meet the cavalry threat. Troops were formed into squares four deep with the front ranks kneeling presenting a wall of bayonets. The Regimental squares were positioned on the northern reverse slope of the ridge in a chequer-board effect and artillery guns were placed along the ridge with the gunners instructed to fall back to the squares for protection when the French cavalry closed with them, resuming their positions at the guns the

French cavalry counter attack the British.

moment it was safe to do so. Finally the Duke placed what was left of his heavy cavalry to the rear, where they were to counter-charge the French as required. For the next few hours the French assaulted the ridge, shot at by artillery on the way up, swirling around the squares like waves around rocks, being counter charged when their formation was lost and being shot at again as they retreated. Twelve times they came forward for this punishment until both men and horses were exhausted. The Duke spent this time during the battle moving around the positions encouraging troops, taking shelter in squares and redirecting artillery as required.

At approximately 6.00pm, the Duke was informed that La Haie-Sainte was about to fall and so he hurried back across to the crossroads to take command of the action in the centre of his line. The fall of the central stronghold was a serious threat to his position and for a period of about 30 minutes, the road to Brussels was clear for the French to advance down. Wellington was now faced with the possibility of defeat and moved every available soldier to cover the centre. By the time Napoleon began to move troops forward, Wellington had closed the window of opportunity that had existed for the French.

At approximately 8.00pm, Napoleon ordered forward the Imperial Guard, Wellington observed the movement and at first must have been concerned that it was going to impact upon his line in that frail area north of La Haie-Sainte. Just to the south of the farmhouse, the Guard swung westwards and began advancing up the slope that the cavalry had been assaulting all afternoon. Wellington was now positioned on the ridge, halfway between La Haie-Sainte and Hougoumont with the Foot Guards of Maitland. As the Imperial Guard crossed the ridge, he ordered the British Guards to stand up and deliver volley fire into their French counter-parts. To the Duke's right, the 52nd Light Infantry under Sir John Colborne advanced, turned on the flank of the Imperial Guard and poured fire into the formation. For the first time in battle, the Imperial Guard broke and began to retreat.

Wellington now ordered the advance of the whole line, telling the commander of the 52nd to 'go on Colborne, go on. They won't stand. Don't give them chance to rally'. Wellington then headed towards the Genappe road, whether along the ridge or due east cross-country is unknown. He was with Uxbridge, however, 'in the low ground to the south of La Haie-Sainte' when his second in command was struck in the knee, losing his leg, the time was approximately 8.30pm. As the whole battle was now heading in a southerly direction, inevitably friendly fire became a problem with units intermingling and Prussian troops now caught up in the chaos. Several senior officers pleaded with Wellington not to go any further forward, but his reply was stoical 'never mind, let them fire away. The battle is gained; my life's of no consequence now.'

Wellington stopped in the vicinity of La Belle Alliance where he met with Blücher at approximately 9.00pm. After the two commanders had embraced, they discussed the details of the pursuit that was to follow. Wellington then halted his exhausted army, let the Prussians continue the pursuit and then slowly rode back to his Head-quarters at Waterloo village.

Analysis of Wellington's performance on 18 June stands up well to even the most intense scrutiny. The simple fact is that he gave a near flawless performance, and when one considers that commanders who make the least mistakes win

This rather grim sketch realistically captures the moment when Blücher met Wellington. 'Mein lieber komrade! Quelle affaire!' was reportedly the expression used by Blücher when the two met.

battles, it becomes obvious that the Allies had a very strong advantage. It is true to say that Wellington was caught short prior to the main battle itself by the speed of the French advance. His army was dispersed over a wide area and had Ney's wing been fully formed, it is doubtful he could have held Quatre Bras. Wellington's deployment of 17,000 troops at Hal to protect him from an attempt to outflank him to the east turned out to be unnecessary, but he was not to know that at the start of the battle. His selection of the defensive position along the Mont St Jean ridge has been criticised by many, including Napoleon himself, but afforded protection

Wellington makes his lonely journey back to Waterloo. The Iron Duke was deeply affected by the high casualty rate.

for his army from both fire and view. Wellington decided to fight on 18 June knowing that the Prussians were moving towards him, and therefore the position he chose was perfect for his purposes. As to his own positioning on the battlefield, it is clear he was always in the right place at the right time. The arched line he adopted allowed for lateral vision, giving him advanced warning of d'Erlon's assault. His behaviour was inspirational throughout, and there can be no better evidence of this than the fact that so many who fought that day reported seeing him in their location, whether that be in a vantage point to observe events or sharing the danger within an infantry square. On 18 June 1815, Wellington was ubiquitous.

Battlefield Walk 1 - In the Footsteps of Wellington

Start the tour of Wellington's movements at Hougoumont (A). Here was fought a battle within a battle and therefore provides an excellent opportunity to look at another element of Waterloo. There are several memorials on the walls and within the grounds of Hougoumont, and the

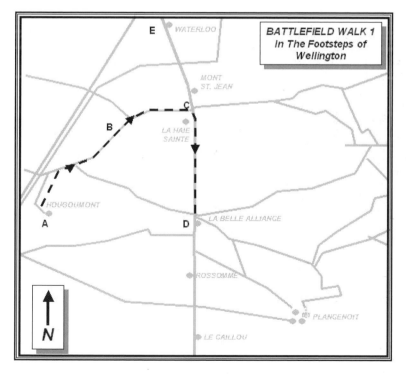

story of the battle here can be told through the description of each at Appendix A and the Hougoumont complex schematic.

From Hougoumont, walk the Hollow Way (sunken ground running south-west to north-east by the edge of the woods opposite the northern walls of Hougoumont) towards the main ridge (B) where Wellington spent much of the battle either observing the assaults on Hougoumont, steadying the squares, directing the Guards or the 52nd Light Infantry. Observe across the valley to the eastern edge of the battlefield and you will be able to appreciate the importance of the 'lateral vision' that the Duke enjoyed from this position. By following the line of site between here and La Belle Alliance and the area to the right of that building is the ground the French cavalry crossed during the ill-fated charges of the afternoon. Memorials to Mercer and Demulder are along this ridge, (the details of which are at Appendix A, memorials 10 and 11), and the location allows you to visualize the forward location of the British guns with the infantry in squares on the reverse slope.

Detail from the Mercer Memorial.

Continue north past the side of the Lion Mound to the road that passes the Visitor Centre and Wax Works Museum, and continue to the crossroads north of La Haie-Sainte (C). Running west from the crossroads is the Ohain or Sunken Road that proved such a formidable obstacle for the French cavalry. It is difficult to imagine now as the soil that was used to build the gargantuan Lion Mound was taken from this area, causing the 'sunken' road to become elevated to ground level. The Gordon Memorial (Appendix A, Memorial 12) gives the visitor some idea of the height of the ground in this area during the battle. Built before the Lion Mound, the Gordon Memorial sits upon the original surface of the battlefield and gives a clear indication of the slope that must of existed from the low ground around La Haie Sainte to the main defensive position on the ridge. The crossroads marked the centre of the Allied line and the point at which Wellington located himself during d'Erlon's assault and after La Haie-Sainte fell. A sycamore tree now grows at the spot where the famous elm tree, used as shelter by Wellington, once stood. The elm was badly damaged by souvenir hunters and it had to be cut down shortly after the battle. It was sold to an Englishman who made a chair from it which was presented to Queen Victoria and is still in the possession of the Royal Family, as well as walking sticks and more conventional souvenirs. Looking south from the crossroads towards the French positions, there are two buildings of interest that sit beside the road. The furthest of these on the left-hand side at the crest of the rise and at a distance of just over a kilometre, is La Belle Alliance and the building on the right hand ride at a distance of 200m or so is La Haie-Sainte. There are a number of memorials in the immediate area of the crossroads and on the eastern wall of La Haie-Sainte refer to Appendix A for details.

Descend from the highpoint at the crossroads in a southerly direction on the Genappe road. Wellington was sighted on this road on his way to meet Blücher at La Belle Alliance (D) and was with Uxbridge in this area when the latter was struck on his leg. There is a memorial on the wall of La Belle Alliance (Appendix A, Memorial 25) commemorating the meeting between the two Army commanders, but the building also marks the furthest south Wellington travelled during the battle. At La Belle Alliance, he turned his horse, Copenhagen, around and rode back alone to Waterloo village. In the village it is worth visiting both Wellington's Headquarters (E) as well as the church opposite that houses many of the British Regimental memorials. The Headquarters contains some interesting relics from the battle including the bed in which Lieutenant Colonel Gordon died and Uxbridge's wooden prosthesis. Wellington spent the night of the 18 June in the room next door to Gordon and was reported by several witnesses to be tearful, something that would not normally be associated with the 'Iron Duke'. Not only had he just fought an extremely stressful battle in which many of his friends had been either killed or wounded as well as the incredibly high casualty rate in his army, but since waking on the 15 June, Wellington had no more than nine hours sleep. He was physically and mentally drained and one can sympathise with his heartfelt statement that he would 'thank God I have fought my last battle'.

La Belle Alliance, the centre of the French Line and the area in which Napoleon spent much of the battle, as it was shortly after Waterloo. (Cruilshank)

La Belle Alliance today.

CHAPTER 16

'NEVER DID NAPOLEON HAVE SO FORMIDABLE OR SO FRAGILE A WEAPON IN HIS HANDS' (NAPOLEON AND NEY AT WATERLOO)

THE FRENCH army was under the direct command of Napoleon, but he in turn had given Ney command of the French Left Wing and thus was the appointed battle-captain when the armies closed on one another. Napoleon spent much of 18 June in a stationary position near La Belle Alliance or resting at Rossomme, whilst Ney was anything but stationary. Much like Wellington, he was to be found at the point of crisis throughout the day, but, unlike Wellington, and with one notable exception, he was unable to grasp the larger context of the battle; he was in the low ground and Wellington on the high ground. Ney was further hampered by Napoleon's presence, appeared unsure of how best to react and knowing that the Emperor could overrule him at any stage. Napoleon did not ease the situation any, and his own lack of dynamism on the 18 June was undoubtedly a contributing factor to the disaster that befell his army. It therefore makes sense to compare and contrast the movements of the two French commanders together rather than as separate identities.

Ney met with Napoleon and other senior generals for breakfast at Le Caillou some time around 8 am, at the time Napoleon was

This interesting portrait by James Sant shows Napoleon looking quite ill and is probably the most realistic image of his appearance at the time of Waterloo that has come down to us.

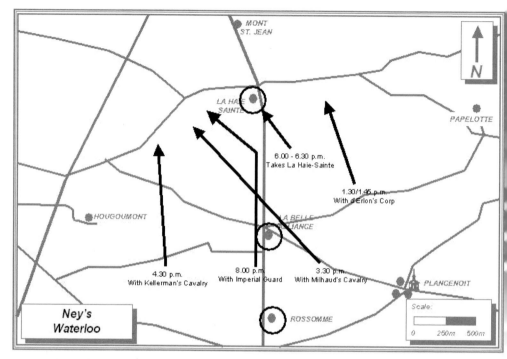

dressing down Soult for praising the British troops and Wellington in particular. Napoleon appeared to be in a buoyant and confident mood, declaring that the whole affair would be over quickly, nothing more than a picnic, and went ahead and ordered his meal for that evening in Brussels. Senior officers who had fought Wellington in the Peninsular implored the Emperor to use manoeuvre rather than frontal assault against Wellington, but Napoleon was to have none of it. Ney offered the extraordinary information that the Allied army was '... in full retreat. They are disappearing into the forest'. Napoleon was unconvinced, merely stating that Ney had 'not seen right'. This would not be the last time that Ney thought Wellington was withdrawing from the field, the second time would have dire consequences. This mistake may have been caused by something far deeper that a simple misinterpretation of some troop movement. Ney was not the Ney of old at Waterloo, something was badly wrong with his personality and judgement and this needs to be examined in more detail. Napoleon was also not his former dynamic self, prompting one senior officer to comment, 'The Napoleon we knew does not exist anymore'. Napoleon was undoubtedly tired and ill, he was under immense pressure to win and win quickly. His confidence was almost certainly not a true reflection of his feelings, but more of an attempt to instil confidence in his subordinate commanders.

As already discussed, there will always remain doubt as to the exact time that the battle commenced, and whilst any delay favoured Wellington, the waste of precious hours that morning did little to damage the French confidence. Ney spent time after breakfast speaking with d'Erlon, probably discussing the battle formation for the advance on Wellington's left and how the battle should proceed once the flank had been turned. Ney then went forward and joined the troops on the line. Napoleon used the time offered by the delay to conduct a review of his army, stiffening resolve amongst the ranks and no doubt inflicting some psychological damage on the exposed brigade of Belgians belonging to Bylandt. Both Napoleon and Ney returned to the area of La Belle Alliance before the commencement of battle at approximately 11.30 am when the diversionary assault on Hougoumont began.

Ney placed himself with d'Erlon during the main engagement of the Grand Battery. Once Ney entered the low ground between the armies at the head of d'Erlon's magnificent Corps, he ceased to function as an effective commander. Rarely venturing from the valley, he immersed himself in the fight, returning to his roots as a trooper, unable to grasp the wider vision of the battle. The grand advance, designed to turn Wellington's left flank, place a Corps between him and Blücher and force a withdrawal towards the coast was a failure. Ney appeared to become ever more desperate as the battle continued, determined to give the Emperor some tangible success, determined to make up for any grievance he had caused by previous comments about 'iron cages'. Napoleon watched the defeat of d'Erlon's Corps from the area of La Belle Alliance with disbelief but hardly a loss of confidence; the chances of victory that he rated at nine to one before the battle he now placed at six to four. He was clearly unwell and retired from the field to the farm of Rossomme to rest.

By mid-afternoon, Ney saw what he thought was the Allied line in retreat, when what he actually saw was Allied troops withdrawing on command to further protect themselves on the reverse slope of Mont St Jean. Ney was, however, convinced and immediately ordered the cavalry forward, initiating the most enduring image of Waterloo; that of French cavalry swarming around Allied infantry squares. If Ney had been correct

Marshal Ney at the head of the French cavalry leads the charges against the Allied squares. (Detail fron the Waterloo panarama)

and Wellington was indeed withdrawing from the battlefield, Ney's orders would have led to the destruction of the Allied army. Infantry retreating would have been smashed beyond recognition by heavy cavalry, the battle would have been won by late afternoon and the probability of a second battle against the Prussians on the 19th the most likely outcome. But Ney was wrong. Napoleon would always hold him responsible for the defeat and his reputation would forever be of a heroic blunderer. Ney was present on all the main charges and although impossible to quantify exactly, it is thought to have been about twelve. Time and again he moved over the ever-deteriorating ground, replacing horses that were shot from under him with those of dead troopers. An epaulette was shot off and yet he still remained unscathed, seemingly detached from the reality of his actions. Napoleon had done absolutely nothing to prevent Ney making the mistake. Having returned to the field as the first wave was about to depart, Napoleon actually reinforced the error, sending forward a second wave, his only comment being that the attack had taken place an hour too early and that now it was underway, the best he could do was support it. Whilst his most celebrated lieutenant was leading the French cavalry to immortality, Napoleon remained in the area of La Belle Alliance, preoccupied with what was now becoming a major source of concern, the pressure of Bülow's Prussians on Plancenoit.

With the cavalry attacks having failed, Ney, probably rather disappointed to find himself still alive, received the order to take La Haie-Sainte at all costs. Gathering what troops he could find, Ney led the final storm that swept into, and this time over, the brave men of the King's German Legion under the command of Major Baring. The farm complex fell at about 6.30 pm, and this was the first exploitable success that Ney, and indeed the French, had enjoyed all day. Ney appeared to come to life again, for the first time he saw clearly and could appreciate the full importance of his immediate success. In front of him, less than 400 yards away, was the battered and barely solid centre of the Allied line. Ney knew that if he could breach the line and pile troops through, the Allies would be split in half, many would panic and again the battle could still be won. Calling forward artillery that inflicted appalling casualties, especially amongst the 27th Inniskilling, Ney sent his Aide-de-Camp (ADC), Colonel Héymes, to ask permission for the release of the Imperial Guard to administer the *coup de grace*. It was

The memorial on the eastern wall of La Haine Sainte commemorating the attack by Marshal Ney in the early evening.

too late. Napoleon was fighting the Prussians at Plancenoit and for the second time, Ney's chance of being the saviour of France was crushed.

Ney left the troops occupying La Haie-Sainte and moved back towards La Belle Alliance. He was probably fuming with Napoleon, but if he remonstrated or even spoke to the Emperor, it was not recorded. In reality it would have been of little value. Wellington had repaired his centre, silenced the guns and the opportunity that Ney had created was lost. For

La Haie-Sainte today is little changed from its 1815 state. The photograph shows the eastern wall and the Brussels-Charleroi road that formed the central axis of the battlefield.

all the courage he had displayed and for the genuine opportunity he had created, his timing was poor. The action needed to have happened several hours earlier, before the Prussians made their presence felt. With Plancenoit now back in French hands, but the Prussians still pressing and arriving in every increasing numbers, Napoleon needed to act fast and, with a final throw of the dice, ordered forward the Imperial Guard against the Allied main line.

Napoleon led the Imperial Guard forward himself, straight down the road from La Belle Alliance towards La Haie-Sainte. At a point just short of La Haie-Sainte, the Guard changed direction and headed left at an oblique angle towards the Allied line, aiming somewhere in vicinity of where the Lion Mound is today. Napoleon did not go forward with them from La Haie-Sainte, but instead retired back to La Belle Alliance where at least he could see and direct the battle. Ney, typically for his performance that day, did stay with the Guard advancing on foot as a fifth horse was shot from under him. As the Guard collapsed under withering fire, and the French army began its panic-stricken flight from the field, Ney remained calm. Time and again he attempted to rally the French, moving from group to group, imploring men to stand with him and 'see how a Marshal of France can die!' One witness recalled seeing Ney hammering his broken sword against the barrel of a cannon in sheer frustration, calling out to d'Erlon to stand otherwise 'we will be hanged if we live through this'. When the darkness eventually fell, Ney was in the company of a loyal corporal who found him a horse and began the trip back to France. Ney was, as he had been on the retreat from Moscow in 1812, the last to quit the field. Unlike in 1812, Waterloo was a field he probably wished he never left.

Napoleon fell back with remnants of the Guard and like Ney was unable to halt the rout that was happening around him. In the area of Rossomme he finally linked up with his carriage and was spirited off the battlefield. When it looked likely that his entourage was to be overrun by Prussians near Genappe, he transferred to a horse and continued his way back to Paris convinced that the battle may have been lost but the war most certainly was not.

If we accept that Napoleon was ill, tired and under pressure, making his performance at Waterloo well below that which had become the norm, how can the performance of Ney be explained? Ney made a number of errors on 18 June and these are quite possibly linked to his mental state. At Quatre Bras he was heard to say, 'if only an English bullet would kill me!' Apart from his own dramatic offer to witness his battlefield death, many observers reported Ney as having 'a death wish' or 'seeking death'. His judgement was clearly clouded and the fact he thought on two occasions the Allies were running away before him is disturbing. Before Waterloo, Ney was famous for his grim humour, offering jokes and encouragement to individuals. There is no evidence of this side of his character at Waterloo. Ney was nothing short of a killing machine, unafraid of death and virtually incapable of making a correct decision.

Napoleon latter commented on Ney's character during the Waterloo campaign saying that he had been 'softened by the events of 1814' and that Ney had 'lost some of that dash, that resolution, and that self-confidence which had won so much glory'. Much as Napoleon was not at his best at Waterloo, the man with whom he placed so much responsibility and trust was probably in a far worse condition.

The first possible explanation is that Ney realized from the moment Napoleon returned from Elba that he was living an impossible dream, that France would never be safe as long as Napoleon was in charge and eventually the country would be overrun and occupied. As a Marshal he would be put to death, if not by the Allies, then certainly by the Bourbons. Death on the battlefield was a preferable option. The soldier in Ney could not however resist one last 'hurrah', one last chance of glory, and one last fight. Although undoubtedly a patriot, for this to be the true state of mind that Michel Ney was in when he joined the Emperor would require him to dispel his faith in ultimate French victory and the display of considerable political foresight, something for which he was not renowned. There exists another possibility that would explain Ney's poor decision making, his change in character and especially his complete disregard for personal safety. A modern psychiatrist would say that these are all classic signs of Post Traumatic Stress Disorder (PTSD), the modern name for battle fatigue or severe cases of battle shock. Napoleon's use of the word 'softened' when describing Ney is interesting, especially in light of the fact that PTSD was not recognized at that time. Ney's desperate search for death on the slopes of Mont St Jean was probably not a selfish final act of unsurpassed glory, more likely an act of despair from a man who had spent his entire adult life fighting and saw nothing beyond the immediate battle for him to live for.

Napoleon was later to blame several individuals for his defeat at Waterloo, most notably Ney. Neither Napoleon nor Ney were at their brilliant best on 18 June but neither helped themselves by their movements around the field. The French army suffered from what Wellington considered to be the art of war, namely 'knowing what was on the other side of the hill'. There exists no record that an attempt was made to find out what was on the other side of the Mont St Jean ridge, and both men positioned themselves on the battlefield where that information could not be gleaned. Napoleon static and detached, Ney submerged in the valley between the two armies, brave to a fault, highly inspirational but, as Napoleon was later to comment:

'Ney forgot the troops who were not under his eye. The bravery that a general-in-chief ought to display is different from that which a divisional general must have, just as the latter's ought not to be the same as that of a

captain of grenadiers.'

Battlefield Walk 2 - In the Footsteps of Napoleon and Ney

Napoleon was largely static during Waterloo whilst Ney was continually moving from one part of the battlefield to another. For those who wish to just gain an appreciation of the view the commanders enjoyed, then one only needs to visit La Belle Alliance. For those who want to gain a more detailed perspective, then it is important to follow Ney into the valley and try to imagine how limited his overall grasp of the situation would have been.

Start the tour of Napoleon and Ney's movements at Le Caillou (A). Here both men rested the night of the 17th and the breakfast meeting was conducted. There is a range of interesting relics within the building and

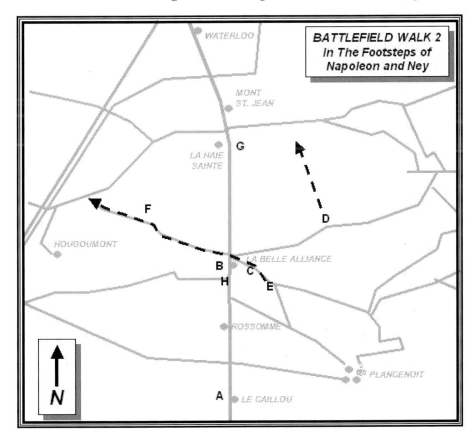

grounds of Le Caillou; the breakfast briefing room has been restored to its original condition and the garden contains a monument of bones that have been recovered from the battlefield over the years.

Moving towards the battlefield itself, you pass by the site of Rossomme, but nothing is left of the building today. Keep going until you reach La Belle Alliance (B) in what was the centre of the French line. Although it is impossible to position Ney with any certainty from after his conference with d'Erlon at Le Caillou, it is most likely that he was in the vicinity of the La Belle Alliance in the immediate period prior to the battle commencing.

Napoleon did not spend the entire battle in the area of La Belle Alliance, as he was at the Rossomme farm house for a fair proportion of the early stages, only moving forward once he sensed his presence was required. If you take the road in a south-easterly direction from La Belle Alliance for 150m, you reach 'Napoleon's Observation Post' (C) at which he may have spent some of the battle. When he did move forward, Napoleon would have positioned himself at the point that offered him the best visibility. It is therefore impossible to place Napoleon other than in the general vicinity of La Belle Alliance. There are several memorials on the walls of La Belle Alliance, details of which are at Appendix A.

Follow the road east from La Belle Alliance and then take the farm track that forks off to the left after about 100m. You are now walking along the

Papelotte and La Haie-Sainte as seen from Durutte's start line on the right of the French line. Durutte led his division with considerable skill during the day, losing his hand towards the latter stages.

The farm complex of Papelotte defended by the Nassau troops anchored Wellington's left. Although parts of the hamlet of La Haie fell in the initial stages of the battle, the flank held firm and was the first to be relieved by the Prussians.

ridge where d'Erlon deployed his Corps (D), Napoleon formed his Grand Battery and behind both of which were the cavalry of Milhaud. Ney made his way from La Belle Alliance to the front of d'Erlon's Corps and from this position you have a grandstand view of the ground over which the French crossed. Ney would have witnessed the disintegration of Bylandt's Belgian brigade and sensed that the time was now right for d'Erlon to strike what was hoped to be the decisive blow, ordered the advance. The slope leading up to Picton's troops is clearly visible although it is not as high or as steep as many contemporary paintings may suggest. To the right of the ridge is the Papelotte farm complex and to the left the complex of La Haie-Sainte, the scene of such fierce fighting throughout the day. If you feel inclined, walk across the fields towards the Allied line and try to imagine not only the utter chaos that must have engulfed d'Erlon's men as

British heavy cavalry crashed into them from behind the ridgeline, but also how isolated from command Ney must have been.

Whilst Napoleon was resting at Rossomme, Ney was full of activity. He was probably around La Belle Alliance when he made the fatal error of assessing the rearward movement of Allied troops as a full-scale withdrawal and decided upon a massed cavalry attack. Follow the road to Plancenoit and where it forks marks the start point of the cavalry attacks (E). Detail of the monument to the 5th Armoured Regiment located at this fork is explained at Appendix A, Memorial 31. The advance crossed the Brussels road near La Belle Alliance and continued towards the ridgeline between Hougoumont and the Lion Mound. As an axis, one can follow the dirt track that cuts across the fields (F). One can easily grasp the sense of surprise that must have gripped Ney when he crossed the ridgeline only to see the formed squares of Allied infantry. More importantly, one can also realize that the couple of hours Ney spent going back and forth with the cavalry were two hours that he had no control or understanding of what as happening elsewhere.

After the attacks exhausted themselves, Ney launched his successful

The main farm house within La Haie-Sainte through which the majority of the 42 survivors from the original compliment of 376 escaped. The rear of the farm house leads out into a garden, where Colonel von Ompteda was killed in an attempt to recapture the complex.

The Wounded Eagle, the primary French memorial on the battlefield today and the site of the destruction of much of the Imperial Guard.

attack on La Haie-Sainte (G). It was about 6 pm when he began the attack, approaching the complex from the south-east, and by 6.30 pm it had fallen. The building has several memorial plaques, including one to the Marshal, details of which are at Appendix A, Memorials 18-22. Napoleon can also be linked to La Haie-Sainte as he advanced this far with the Imperial Guard before turning back. The best way to approach the farm complex is from the south, from La Belle Alliance. After 75m on the right, there is a monument to the 6th Foot Artillery (Appendix A, Memorial 24); this marked the left hand edge of the Grand Battery that pummelled the Allied lines for so much of the day. Napoleon advanced down the road with the guard at about 7.30 pm, and must have linked up with Ney somewhere along the route. At La Haie-Sainte the Guard swung towards the Lion Mound and Ney accompanied it until it was destroyed and broke. By this stage, probably 8.30 pm, Napoleon was back at La Belle Alliance.

The movements of Napoleon and Ney in the chaotic route of the French Army are hard to trace. Napoleon was escorted for much of the time by the remains of the Imperial Guard. The Guard fell back south of La Belle Alliance and was largely destroyed in the area of the French Memorial, 'The Wounded Eagle' (H) (Appendix A, Memorial 37). Near this area he transferred to his coach and withdrew to Genappe where he was nearly captured by Prussians in the gridlock of routed troops. Napoleon transferred to a horse and escaped ahead of his men to Paris.

Ney conducted his own fighting withdrawal and was typically one of the last off the field. He was exhausted, ragged in appearance and certainly humiliated, his personal pride in much the same state as his once immaculate uniform. He borrowed a horse and worked his way back to Paris via Marchienne, Beaumont and Avesnes.

APPENDIX A

CONSOLIDATED LIST OF BATTLEFIELD MEMORIALS

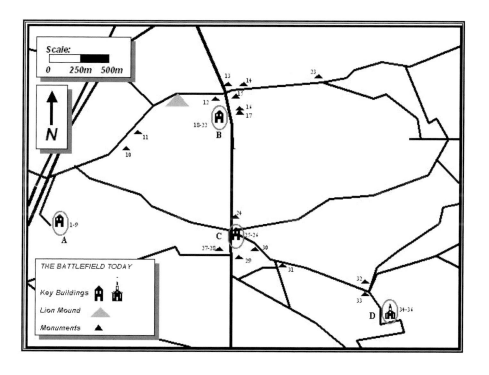

A. Hougoumont

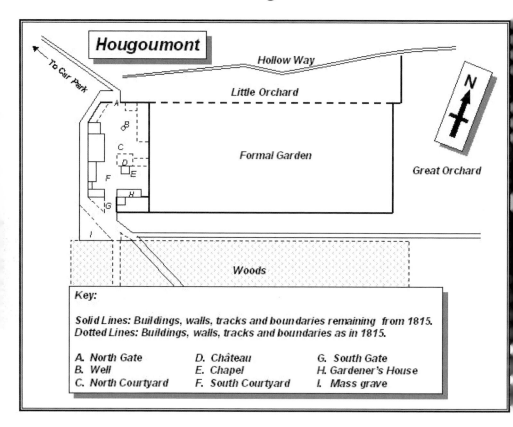

Key:

Solid Lines: Buildings, walls, tracks and boundaries remaining from 1815.
Dotted Lines: Buildings, walls, tracks and boundaries as in 1815.

A. North Gate	D. Château	G. South Gate
B. Well	E. Chapel	H. Gardener's House
C. North Courtyard	F. South Courtyard	I. Mass grave

The North Gate

The fighting at the North Gate was fierce, particularly so when soldiers from the French 1st Light Infantry Regiment broke into the courtyard. Lieutenant Legros, a huge axe-wielding pioneer officer, led the thirty or forty Frenchmen that entered through the North Gate. In the bitter hand-to-hand fighting that followed, only an unarmed drummer boy survived, Legros being cut down by a sword thrust behind his knee and finished with bayonets. The North Gate had been left open as a means to resupply the garrison, but the French had used the west wall as cover and had advanced around the outside. Lieutenant Colonel James Macdonell,

The appraoch to the North Gate showing the western wall of Hougoumont. French troops briefly entered the complex through this gate.

commanding the garrison in the main part of the complex, was alerted to the danger of the gates being open and the French assaulting through his line of communication with the rest of the army. Along with five other Guardsmen, he pushed the gate shut and barred it from the mass of Frenchmen tying to force entry. The walls around the North Gate are not as high today as they were during the battle, and the gate itself is considerably less substantial.

1. Scots Guards Memorial

Beside the North Gate there is a plaque dedicated to the Scots Guards (3rd Regiment of Foot Guards). The Light Company of the Regiment, commanded by Lieutenant Colonel Charles Dashwood, bore the brunt of the second French attack. Positioned to the west of the complex, the Guardsmen were driven back and entered Hougoumont through the North Gate.

2. Royal Wagon Train Memorial

On the wall of the barn on the right as you enter through the North Gate, is a plaque dedicated to the men of the Royal Wagon Train. The garrison needed to be resupplied throughout the day with ammunition, and this task befell the logisticians of The Royal Wagon Train. The most intriguing incident involving these men centred on Private or Corporal Brewer or Brewster. This brave man drove his train to the North Gate, despite the heavy shellfire and the danger posed by the fires in Hougoumont, where his horses were killed. The ammunition reached the Guardsmen and Brewer or Brewster remained to help in the defence. He was later said to have transferred to the Scots Guards, but the regimental historians can find no record of this.

3. The Chapel

Inside the courtyard area remains the only existing part of the old château, the Chapel. Many of the wounded were brought to the Chapel to protect them from the fire and bullets that swept the courtyard. Once the château caught fire, it seemed only a matter of time before the flames engulfed the Chapel, but for some extraordinary reason the flames came no further than the door. On the inside of the door hung a fifteenth century wooden image of Christ on the Cross; the flames reached the feet of Christ where they promptly stopped and retreated. The Crucifix is now on the wall of the

The Chapel at Hougoumont where the wounded were sheltered during the fighting.

The crucifix that hung on the inside of the chapel door. When the fire spread from the chateau, the flames came under the door then retreated when they licked at the feet of the image. Scorch marks can still be clearly seen.

Chapel, but the scorch marks on the feet can still be seen. On the exterior wall of the Chapel is a bronze plaque to commemorate those who died defending Hougoumont, dedicated by The Brigade of Guards.

4. Grenadier Guards Memorial
On the exterior wall of the Chapel facing the Formal Garden (now a paddock) is a plaque dedicated to the Grenadier Guards (1st Regiment of Foot Guards). The detachment from the 1st Guards, commanded by Lieutenant Colonel Lord Alexander Saltourn, was responsible for holding the Great Orchard beyond the walls of the Formal Garden. The orchard changed hands several times during the battle and was the scene of furious attacks and counter-attacks.

The South Gate
The French made their first attack against the South Gate, advancing in contact with Hanoverian and Nassauer troops through the wood that was separated from the complex by a farm track. The wood was severely damaged during the fighting, many of the trees dying as a result. Today, three trees still stand and mark the northern boundary of the wood

View from the South Gate of Hougoumont. The three trees are all that remain of the wood through which the French advanced at the start of the battle. To the right of the trees is a large, unmarked mass grave that contains the remains of defenders and attackers from 18 June 1815.

The digging of the mass grave in front of the South Gate of Hougoumont. The grave is recorded as containing 300 British and 800 French dead. (Dighton)

opposite the South Gate. The first attack by Prince Jerome's Division was spearheaded by General Bauduin's Brigade, and was defeated with heavy loss of life, including that of the Brigade Commander. Along the wall running down the outside of the Formal Garden, one can still see the loopholes cut by the defenders and the scars left by the fighting. After the battle, a large mass grave was dug in the open ground between the South Gate and the three remaining trees. The grave is unmarked, but is recorded as containing the bodies of 300 British and 800 French. The British are known to have suffered 1,500 casualties and the French some 5,000. If you accept that the wounded normally outnumbered those killed by at least four to one, it would appear that the majority of those killed are therefore buried in this unmarked grave.

5. Coldstream Guards Memorial

On the wall next to the South Gate is a plaque dedicated to the Coldstream Guards (2nd Regiment of Foot Guards). The detachment from the Regiment, commanded by Lieutenant Colonel Macdonell of North Gate fame, held the château complex and Formal Garden. Apart from the brief incursion through the North Gate, French soldiers failed to gain a foothold in the areas defended by the Coldstream Guards.

6. General Bauduin Memorial

On the south facing wall by the Gardeners Cottage is a plaque in French dedicated to General Bauduin; its translation reads as: *In memory of General Bauduin who fell in front of these walls on 18 June 1815.* General Bauduin led the first French attack that assaulted the South Gate.

The Formal Garden

Confusion exists with visitors as to the location of the Formal Garden in relation to the Great Orchard; this is of significance as the French did not manage to enter the garden, but held the orchard for periods during the day. The garden is now a paddock, ringed with the original wall. The orchard no longer exists, but was located on the eastern side of the garden wall.

Loopholes cut by British Guardsmen during the night 17 June and from which they fired upon the French assaults the following day.

7. Graves of Captain Blackman and Sergeant-Major Cotton

In the garden there are two gravestones marking the original site of the graves of Captain John Lucie Blackman and Sergeant-Major Edward Cotton. Blackman was killed fighting with the Coldstream Guards during the defence of Hougoumont. Cotton was serving with the 7th Hussars during the battle and survived to set up the Hôtel du Musée, now the Wax Works Museum opposite the Visitor Centre. He made his living after the battle as a guide and was the author of *A Voice From Waterloo*. The bodies were exhumed in 1890 and moved to the new British cemetery for those killed at Waterloo in Evere, Brussels.

The graves within the Formal Garden belonging to Captain Blackman, killed in the defence of Hougoumont and Sergeant Major Cotton who survived the battle and became a celebrated battlefield guide.

8. Craufurd Memorial

A white stone plaque in the interior wall of the garden remembers Captain Thomas Craufurd of the Scots Guards, killed during the defence of Hougoumont.

9. French Memorial

A memorial to the French killed during the attacks on Hougoumont can be found near the eastern wall of the garden. The inscription can be translated as: *To the French who died at Hougoumont on 18 June 1815.* Underneath the main inscription is a second sentence, attributed to Napoleon whilst on St. Helena, that can be translated as: *The earth seemed proud to carry so many brave men.*

The positioning of the memorial is quite extraordinary as it is within the garden, the part of the Hougoumont complex which the French did not penetrate. The historically correct location for the memorial would be on the other side of the wall, in the site of the former orchard. One must assume that the reason for this memorial being sited at this location is to make homage easier for the visitor; ironically the only 'brave men' who are in the earth here are their enemy!

The French memorial in the garden at Hougoumont. Ironically, no Frenchman reached this far into the complex.

10. Memorial to Captain Mercer

Captain Cavalié Mercer of the Royal Horse Artillery was moved to this location by Wellington himself after the first French cavalry attack, and remained at his guns throughout the onslaught. As the cavalry closed in on the infantry squares, the artillerymen were to retreat into the nearest square and remain there in relative safety until the attack had been beaten off. As the cavalry withdrew, the artillerymen would return to their guns and pour fire into the retreating cavalry. Mercer was located between two regiments of Brunswickers, who he thought to be unsteady, and deduced that if his men ran back to the squares, the Brunswickers would take example from this backward step and break formation. This was probably a harsh opinion, but as the French dead formed a natural barrier around his guns, Mercer decided that his men would remain at their posts throughout and serve as a moral example to those around them. Mercer came under intense counter-battery fire during this period and was rescued by the quick action of a Dutch battery that identified the source of Mercer's discomfort. Mercer lived into his eighties and eventually retired having attained General rank.

11. Memorial to Lieutenant Demulder

Lieutenant Augustin Demulder was a Belgian serving in Napoleon's army, and was thirty years old at the time of his death. He had begun his final charge with the rest of the 5th Cuirassiers (or 5th Armoured Regiment) from the vicinity of Memorial 31 in the area between La Belle Alliance and Plancenoit, and died within a few kilometres of his family home in Nivelles.

The translation of his memorial is as follows:

In memory of Lieutenant Augustin Demulder of the 5th Cuirassiers. Born in Nivelles, Brabant, in 1785. Knight of the Legion of Honour, wounded in Eylau, 1807, in Essling, 1809, in Hanau, 1813, killed at Waterloo. And also in memory of all the cavalrymen who charged with him on 18 June 1815. The Waterloo Committee in association with the Belgian Society for Napoleonic Studies erected this stone, 1986.

Some local guides translate the wording on the memorial from 5th Cuirassiers to 5th Armoured Division. The 5th Cavalry Division was commanded by Baron Subervie and during the great cavalry charges was engaged against the Prussians on the far side of the battlefield. The 5th Cavalry Division consisted of Hussars and Lancers and was therefore light cavalry, unlikely to be credited with the title 'Armoured'.

Lieutenant Demulder was with the 5th Cuirassiers and therefore any translation that replaces Cuirassier with *Armoured* should read *Regiment* not *Division*. The mistake is probably the result of General HJ Couvreurs *Le drama belge de Waterloo* (Waterloo's Belgian Tragedy); in one particularly flowery passage he refers to Demulder as being from the 5th Armoured Division.

From this ridge, you can appreciate the blind loyalty and courage of the French cavalry. Whereas the British Guardsmen at Hougoumont had to deal with the fear of isolation, the French cavalry had to cope with the shock of crossing the ridge only to find unbroken infantry and then the knowledge of what to expect as they returned through the artillery maelstrom eleven times.

12. The Gordon Memorial

To the south of the crossroads on the right hand side is the memorial to Lieutenant Colonel Sir Alexander Gordon. Gordon was ADC to Wellington and was wounded by a cannonball to his leg towards the end of the battle near the area now occupied by the Lion Mound. He was carried off the field to Waterloo village where he underwent amputation.

After the battle, Wellington went back to his headquarters in Waterloo, he sat by the fire and wrote his famous dispatch and in the early hours went to sleep on the floor having made himself a mattress with some dry straw. At Wellington's request, Gordon occupied the Duke's bed in order that the faithful ADC died in as much comfort as was possible; he was twenty-nine years of age. The monument was built by the Gordon family in 1817 and one of the first to be erected on the battlefield.

13. The Belgian Memorial

On the northeastern corner of the crossroads is the Belgian Memorial. Although Belgium did not exist as an independent country until 1830 (at the time of the battle it was part of the Kingdom of the Netherlands) the Belgians considered themselves a separate identity to the Dutch. Waterloo itself is in French speaking Wallonia, and local inhabitants fought on both sides at the battle. Indeed, it should be remembered that the Belgian people would have to live with the victors of the battle, whether they be Dutch or French and therefore it was important to choose carefully which side you fought upon. The monument was raised in 1914 and commemorates the Belgians who lost their lives fighting for 'the defence of the flag and the honour of arms.' Those Belgians killed at Ligny are also remembered on the monument.

14. The 27th (Inniskilling) Memorial

Situated on the Rue de la Croix, 20m from the junction with the crossroads, stands a simple memorial stone to the Irish soldiers of the 27th (Inniskilling) Regiment of Foot. The inscription is testimony to the courage and sacrifice made by these men as they held the centre of the Allied line together, firstly in the defeat of d'Erlon's attack and then after La Haie-Sainte fell. Of the 747 men that took to the field on the morning of

Detail from the 27th Inniskilling Memorial.

18 June, only 254 were left standing when the battle was over. Most of the casualties were caused by the guns of Napoleon's Grand Battery that were situated on the ridge running opposite the Rue de la Croix.

15. Picton Memorial

Sir Thomas Picton was a true 'soldier's soldier' of the Napoleonic Wars. He was killed leading his Division forward to meet d'Erlon's Corps when a bullet struck his temple shortly after 2.00 pm. His final words were to the Gordon Highlanders, reeling from a devastating volley from the lead French units, 'Rally the Highlanders'. They did and the attack was repulsed.

16. The Hanoverian Memorial

Opposite the Gordon Memorial and La Haie-Sainte is a memorial to the Hanoverian soldiers killed during the battle around the farmhouse and the crossroads. The memorial lists the names of forty-two officers that are buried under the monument, but it is also believed that there are approximately 4,000 other bodies buried here and a large number of horses. Although repatriation of servicemen killed in battle has become more common in today's armies, the British still maintain the tradition of burying their comrades where they fall. In 1815, it was customary to bury the slain in mass graves or burn the bodies on the battlefield; with the sheer numbers involved, it was impractical to do otherwise.

17. The Memorial to Durutte's Division

Next to the Hanoverian memorial is a French language memorial which translates as:

> At this place on 18 June 1815 the 8th Line Infantry regiment of Durutte's Division successfully attacked the 2nd King's German Legion of Colonel von Ompteda.

The 8th had been fighting for much of the day on the eastern edge of the battlefield, and were only called into the centre when Ney prepared his assault on La Haie-Sainte. Colonel von Ompteda was killed leading a counter-attack on La Haie-Sainte which was decimated by French Cuirassiers. The cavalry were assisted in their gruesome task by the 54th and 55th Line Regiments of Quiot's 1st Infantry Division and the 8th Line Regiment from Durutte's Division. Von Ompteda's body was found the next day with a musket ball in his neck, evidently fired from close range as the skin around the entry wound had considerable powder burns.

B. La Haie-Sainte

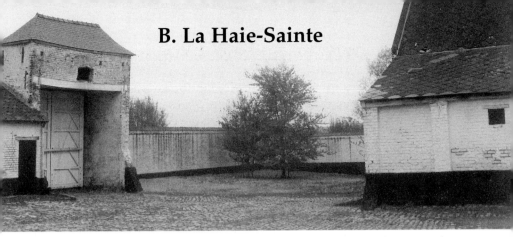

When a dangerous fire broke out at La Haie-Sainte soldiers used water from a pond to put it out. The pond is long gone, but the tree in the picture grows over the site.

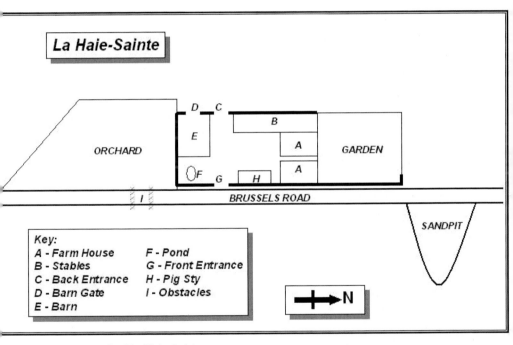

La Haie-Sainte

ORCHARD

D   C
E
F   G
B
A
A
H
GARDEN

BRUSSELS ROAD

I

SANDPIT

Key:
A - Farm House   F - Pond
B - Stables   G - Front Entrance
C - Back Entrance   H - Pig Sty
D - Barn Gate   I - Obstacles
E - Barn

N

The western wall of La Haie-Sainte.

17 June had seen heavy downpours and during the night of 17/18 June it had rained incessantly. Consequently, the 376 men of Major Baring's 2nd Light Battalion, King's German Legion, were wet, cold and hungry when they occupied La Haie-Sainte on the evening of 17 June. In an attempt to dry out and keep warm, many of the doors, including the barn door that was on the western side of the farm, were burnt as firewood. Baring was informed on the morning of 18 June that his battalion would be responsible for conducting the defence of La Haie-Sainte and he now faced the problem of preparing the complex. Baring's carpenters had been sent to Hougoumont, his tools had been lost and there was a gaping hole in the western wall as a result of the barn door being destroyed. His troops therefore cut loopholes with bayonets, used tables from the farmhouse to fashion firing platforms and built barricades along the Brussels road with trees from the orchard. Baring placed three companies in the orchard, two in the farm buildings and courtyard and his remaining company in the garden. In the area of the sandpit opposite the garden were detachments from the 95th Rifles.

Throughout the day, La Haie-Sainte was the focus of repeated French assaults, and not surprisingly, the main effort invariably concentrated on the barn entrance on the western wall. At one stage, the French set fire to the barn, but the danger was extinguished by using the water from the pond carried in cooking pots. Baring was reinforced twice during the

The western gate of La Haie-Sainte through which the French eventually forced entry to the complex. At the time of the entry most of the defenders had run out of ammunition, but still fought back with rifle butts and bayonets.

battle, firstly by two companies from the 1st KGL whom he positioned in the garden and then by two companies of Nassauers. On three occasions, Baring requested an ammunition resupply. The KGL were issued with the Baker Rifle, which used a different type of ammunition to the standard Brown Bess issued to British infantry. Unfortunately for Baring, the ammunition cart carrying the required bullets had overturned, and therefore the requests that he sent went unanswered.

By 6.00 pm Baring and his men were down to approximately four rounds per man. The barn door was barricaded with French dead, most of the KGL soldiers had been killed or wounded and Baring was reaching the limit of what was humanly possible to achieve in the defence of La Haie-Sainte. The end came when Ney launched his final attack on the Allied centre. Despite using bayonets and rifle butts, the KGL were forced to retire through the house and garden and back to the crossroads. Baring himself was one of only forty-two survivors from his original compliment of 376. Colonel Christian von Ompteda, commanding the KGL in the immediate area of the crossroads, launched a brave counter-attack. On the orders of the young and inexperienced Prince of Orange, von Ompteda advanced in line formation against his better judgement and the two battalions he led forward were decimated when French Cuirassiers attacked them from the side. Von Ompteda was last seen alive on his horse, jumping the hedge at the rear of the farmhouse garden; a single bullet through his neck killed him. The French had possession of the key stronghold in the centre of Wellington's position, its loss caused panic in the Allied ranks and for an hour it seemed as though all the French had to do was advance up the road and on to Brussels. Napoleon refused Ney's request for infantry in order to exploit the opportunity created, and by the time the reserves were released Wellington had repaired the hole in his line and the battle was saved.

There are five plaques adorning the farmhouse, all on the eastern wall running beside the Brussels road.

18. General Information: A plaque in four languages by the Front Gate states: *La Haie-Sainte, defended by the King's German Legion, captured by the French infantry at 6 pm.* To complete the story, the 1st (Royal Scots) Regiment of Foot from Picton's Division recaptured the farmhouse as the general advance took place at the end of the battle.

19. 2nd Light Battalion, King's German Legion: On the high gable wall there is a black diamond made of iron that commemorates the officers and men of the 2nd Light Battalion, KGL, who fell in the defence of La Haie-Sainte.

20. *Major Baring and Colonel von Ompteda:* A plaque donated by the citizens of Bexhill-on-Sea, a former KGL garrison is dedicated to the memory of Major Baring and Colonel von Ompteda, and can be found on the garden wall. Whilst the gallant von Ompteda was killed, the equally gallant and bloody-minded Major Baring survived the day, eventually retiring as a Major General in the Hanovarian forces.

21. *French Memorial:* A plaque dedicated to all the French soldiers who died in the attacks on La Haie-Sainte is located next to the Front Gate and can be translated as: *In memory of the French combatants who heroically sacrificed themselves in front of the walls of La Haie-Sainte on 18 June 1815.*

22. *Ney Memorial:* A marbled plaque next to the French Memorial can be translated as: *On 18 June 1815 at around 1830h, the farm of La Haie-Sainte was taken by Marshal Ney thanks to the Heroic assaults of the Sappers of Colonel Lamare's 1st Regiment of Engineers, 2nd Battalion, 2nd Company and the 13th Light Infantry regiment of Donzelot's Division.*

23. *The 21st Line Regiment Memorial*
The memorial marks the high water mark of d'Erlon's attack, originally designed to blast Picton from the ridge, then turn in towards the crossroads, and roll up the Allied army. It also marks the point at which the battle on this side of the field can be best imagined. The inscription can be translated as: *At this place on 18 June 1815 the 21st Line Infantry Regiment of the Marcognet's Division heroically attacked the Anglo-Scottish units for Major-General Pack's brigade.*

24. *6th Foot Artillery*
75m north of La Belle Alliance on the eastern edge of the Brussels road is a monument to the French 6th Foot Artillery. This was the position adopted by the Regiment as part of the Grand Battery and held throughout the day. The inscription can be translated as: *From La Belle Alliance to Papelotte on 18 June 1815, units of Colonel Hulot's 6th Foot Artillery Regiment supported with effective fire the attacks of the 1st French Corps.* This regiment can credit itself with inflicting immense damage on the Allied centre, causing considerable casualties, especially amongst regiments like the 27th (Inniskilling) Regiment of Foot.

C. La Belle Alliance

La Belle Alliance marked the point at which Napoleon halted on the evening of 17 June when following up the retreating Allies from Quatre Bras; the French troops fanned out left and right and thus the building became the centre of the French Line. Napoleon was in the vicinity of La Belle Alliance for much of the day of 18 June, and the building also hosted the historic meeting between Wellington and Blücher at about 9 pm. La Belle Alliance is therefore the only building on the battlefield that can be connected with all three army commanders and was even suggested as the title for the battle by the Prussians. Most importantly, La Belle Alliance provided a reference point for many of the witnesses to the events of 18 June 1815 and therefore it has been easier for the various accounts to be linked to provide an accurate record of the battle. There are two memorials on the building itself, one (25) to the meeting of Wellington and Blücher, the other (26) to the French Medical Services. Although it is probable that wounded were treated here, the position is too far forward to have been safe to use as the main casualty reception and treatment point. The majority of French wounded were taken rearwards for treatment at the Rossomme Farm house, which no longer exists. The memorial can be translated as: *In memory of the French Medical Corps who attended to the wounded with devotion on 18 June 1815.*

It is interesting to note that the medical technique of 'triage' or 'to sort' multiple casualties into a priority of treatment was developed by Napoleon's surgeons. Unlike a civilian hospital, the least badly wounded were often treated first in order to return them to the action as soon as possible. Badly wounded soldiers were usually destined to die and surgeons could do little more than extend their lives by a matter of a few painful hours. The French army, under the guidance of Napoleon's chief surgeon Baron Larrey, enjoyed the comfort of being the first army to have dedicated ambulances that brought casualties to field hospitals from the point of wounding.

27. The French Memorial or 'The Wounded Eagle'
Despite the profusion of French memorials that now can be found on the battlefield, there was no formal memorial before 1904. The battle was a crushing defeat for the French, and therefore was not celebrated by the nation. Despite this, the fact remains that the French army performed magnificently, and was eventually overwhelmed by the combined armies

of Wellington and Blücher. Many brave men were killed in the action and it was only fitting that a memorial to those men should be erected at a suitable site on the battlefield.

The memorial takes the form of a wounded Imperial Eagle carrying a Tricolore in its talons, mounted on a plinth and enclosed by iron railings decorated with flaming grenades and Imperial N's. The dedication on the stone plinth can be translated as: *To the last combatants of the Grand Army, 18 June 1815.* It is a memorial to all those who fought that day, but the reference to 'the last combatants' is intriguing. The Imperial Guard was the only unit to hold any cohesion at the end of the day, and began to withdraw from the field in square formation. As the squares beat off repeated attacks, casualties meant that the squares became triangles and eventually sad, bloody groups of men. It is in this area that part of the Guard was eventually overwhelmed and crushed. It has been suggested that the Wounded Eagle is a memorial to the Imperial Guard because of its location and reference, but this is not the case, and it is a memorial to all of Napoleon's troops.

28. Memorial to the Polish Squadron

Located within the fencing of the Wounded Eagle is a simple memorial to the Polish Squadron. Napoleon had within his army, and indeed within the Guard, Polish troops who formed élite squadrons of lancers. This memorial has an inscription that can be translated as: *In memory of the officers, non-commissioned officers and soldiers of the Polish Squadron who fell at Mont St Jean on 18 June 1815.* It is fitting that these loyal troops have their memorial co-located with the Wounded Eagle. Mont-St-Jean was the name used by the French for Waterloo until recently, following Napoleon's habit of naming battles after his objective.

29. Victor Hugo Monument

The monument to Victor Hugo, author of the epic *Les Misérables*, is to most British, Dutch and German thinking inappropriately placed on the battlefield, as he took no part in the events of 18 June 1815. To the French, and to a surprising degree the Belgians, Hugo was an important man in the context of acceptance of defeat. Raised by an initiative from a Brussels-based non-profit making association, The Victor Hugo Committee, to commemorate his life, it was not completed due to the outbreak of the First World War in 1914. For many years after Waterloo, the French population was numbed by the defeat of Napoleon and the collapse of the

Empire. To add insult to injury, the 'old enemy' Britain secured the lion's share of the benefits of French defeat and became the most powerful nation in the world, effectively the nineteenth century super-power. Victor Hugo lived in Mont St Jean during his exile from France for opposing the reign of Napoleon III. During this time, he wrote his greatest work, the central theme of which was that there was enough glory to go around for all to share, thus making defeat easier for the French to accept. He glorified the battle and heaped praise for the courage shown by the participants, even if his account was riddled with inaccuracies. One of Hugo's claims was that 300 bodies were thrown into the well at Hougoumont with 'the faint cries of those not yet dead haunting the memory'. Not only did this paint an inhumane picture of the British Guardsmen's actions after the battle, but it was patently untrue; a mass grave was dug outside the South Gate and 1,100 soldiers killed in and around Hougoumont were recorded as being buried there. However, Hugo's word had become lore and the well was excavated in 1985; to great surprise only a few animal bones were found. Sadly, Hugo seems to carry some weight as a historian and is still revered by Napoleon's apologists, principally because the glorious account shields Napoleon from the hard analysis that he was the author of his own downfall.

A great writer though he was, it is hard to justify his place alongside the combatants at Waterloo.

30. Napoleon's Observation Post
Take the road in a south-eastern direction from La Belle Alliance for 150m before reaching Napoleon's Observation Post on the right hand side. Napoleon did not spend the entire battle in the area of La Belle Alliance, as he was at the Rossomme Farm house in the early stages, only moving forward once he sensed his presence was required. The location seems slightly odd, as although it provided excellent views of the attack by d'Erlon, the same could not be said of subsequent action, mainly on the western side of the battlefield. Some witnesses have located Napoleon near the Wounded Eagle, others at La Belle Alliance itself. Napoleon was unwell at Waterloo and certainly lacked the vigour of his previous battles, spending large portions of the day at Rossomme, a kilometre behind the line and effectively out of touch with events. When he did move forward, Napoleon positioned himself at the point that offered him the best visibility. It is probable that he was in this location for part of the battle, although it is impossible to put an accurate time to this.

31. *Memorial to 5th Armoured (Cuirassier) Regiment*

Continue along the road towards Plancenoit until you come to a fork in the road. This was the general area in which Milhaud's cavalry was held during the early stages of the battle. Where the road divides, there is a memorial to the French 5th Armoured Regiment. The troops of this Regiment had witnessed the destruction of d'Erlon's Corps and the barrage deposited upon the Allied infantry; they were then told that the Allied army was retreating. Confidence must have been high at the thought of putting the shattered enemy to the sword and made more desirable by the prospect of avenging the carnage inflicted on their fellow countrymen by the British cavalry. Their chance came when Marshal Ney ordered the first of the massed cavalry attacks to commence, and it is from this point that the 5th Armoured Regiment crossed the start line to begin their ill-fated attack. Within two hours, they would cease to exist as a cohesive fighting force.

This monument is directly linked to the Demulder Memorial (No. 11) as the two memorials mark the point at which Demulder began his last charge and where he fell.

The term 'Armoured Regiment' is that given on the memorial stone to the 5th Cuirassiers. The title 'Armoured' refers to the fact that they wore steel helmets and a cuirasse, or breast and back plate. This throwback to earlier times was useful against swords and bayonets, but provided little protection against ballistic wounding, particularly artillery. This is graphically illustrated in the Wellington Museum entrance foyer where there is a breastplate with a hole torn through it, probably by grapeshot. Once thrown from his horse, the movement of the cavalryman was greatly hindered by the armour and was often discarded. Interestingly, the British soldiers found the cuirasse an excellent utensil upon which to fry horsemeat!

The Prussian memorial at Plancenoit. The pressure put on this village by Bülow ensured that Napoleon was distracted and unable to release troops when requested by Ney to exploit the weakness in the Allied centre.

32. The Prussian Memorial

The memorial to the Prussians in Plancenoit commemorates all those who were killed on 18 June 1815 and not just those of Bülow's Corps who fought to take the village itself. Erected in 1819, the dedication can be translated as:

> *To the dead heroes from a Grateful King and Fatherland. May they rest in peace. La Belle Alliance, 18 June 1815.*

It is interesting to note that the Prussians refer to the battle as La Belle Alliance, a fitting title evoking the relationship between Wellington and Blücher taken from the name of the building at which they met at the end of the battle. Wellington stuck to his Peninsular War habit of naming the battle after the location of his Head Quarters, hence Waterloo.

33. Memorial to the Young Guard

At the roundabout near the Prussian Memorial is a memorial to the Young Guard element of the Imperial Guard, led by General Duhesme. The Young Guard fought alongside the Comte de Lobau's Corps against incredible odds as Blücher and Bülow committed battalion after battalion to the fight at Plancenoit. The Young Guard and Lobau were eventually overwhelmed, but were rescued by two battalions of the Old Guard who recaptured the village at bayonet point.

D. The Church at Plancenoit

The church at Plancenoit was the focus of much of the fighting between the Prussians and the French in this sector of the battlefield, and consequently has several memorials around it. Lobau moved to occupy the village once it became apparent that the Prussians were going to support Wellington, and

The church at Plancenoit where heavy fighting took place between the Young Guard and Bülow's Prussians.

were reinforced once the fight was underway by the Young Guard, under the command of General Duhesme. The Prussians, commanded by Bülow, were determined to avenge not only the defeat at Wavre on the 16 June, but also all the other humiliations that Napoleon had inflicted upon them. The battle for control of Plancenoit was therefore vicious and violent in the extreme, no quarter was asked for or given by either side. There are several French memorials situated around the church.

34. Plaque to Duhesme
On the front of the church there is a plaque in French that can be translated as: *In the village of Plancenoit the Young Guard of the Emperor Napoleon distinguished itself on 18 June 1815. It was commanded by General Count Duhesme who was mortally wounded here.*

35. Plaque to M Louis
On the left hand side of the door is another French plaque that can be translated as: *In memory of M Louis, 3rd Guards Infantry, born 3 March 1787, killed at Plancenoit 18 June 1815.*

36. 5th Line Infantry Memorial
At the rear of the church, on a wall of a small chapel, is another plaque to commemorate the actions of the 5th Regiment of Line Infantry, part of Lobau's Corps. The fighting was particularly heavy in this area and the 5th Regiment took correspondingly heavy casualties. The translation of the plaque is as follows: *It was here that on 18 June 1815, the 5th Line Regiment of Simmer's Division, commanded by Colonel Roussille, heroically confronted General Von Bülow's Prussian Corps.*

The 5th Line Infantry were amongst the first troops to confront Napoleon when he returned to France from Elba. Napoleon met them with the words 'Soldiers of the 5th, would you kill your Emperor?' The 5th Line Infantry, along with the 7th Line Infantry were the first to reinforce Napoleons original army of 1,000 men.

APPENDIX B

OTHER PRINCIPAL PERSONALITIES AT WATERLOO

Blücher, Gebhard Leberecht, Prince of Wahlstadt 1742-1819

Born 1742, Blücher was seventy-two years of age when he led the Prussian Army at Waterloo. A former cavalry officer, Blücher had a reputation as a man of extreme courage but limited tactical ability, and was aided throughout the Waterloo campaign by the highly competent but prickly Gneisenau. Blücher was driven by his hatred of Napoleon and a desire for revenge for the humiliations that had been heaped upon his nation by the French Emperor; sentiments that he successfully passed on to his soldiers. Whilst leading a cavalry charge Blücher was wounded and nearly captured when his horse was killed under him at Ligny. Despite his discomfort, he requested that he be tied upright in his saddle during the advance to Waterloo. He trusted Wellington more than most of his compatriots, and this trust was the basis upon which Wellington decided to fight on the morning of 18 June. Blücher met with Wellington at La Belle Alliance, probably at about 9.00 pm, where he greeted his fellow commanding general with what is thought to be the limit of his French: 'Mein Liebe Kamerad, quelle affaire!'

This print of Blucher clearly shows steely determination that manifested itself at Waterloo as he drove his army from Wavre.

Bülow, Friedrich Wilhelm, Graf von Dennewitz 1755-1816

At the start of the Waterloo Campaign, Bülow's 32,000 strong Corps was in Liège. Bülow was senior in rank to Gneisenau, the powerful Chief of Staff, and this caused friction between the two men. Bülow's Corps was effectively independent. This caused Gneisenau to 'request' in his orders rather than 'demand', and by definition a request lacks the urgency of an order. Because of this arrangement, Bülow was unaware of the importance of speed when he was requested to move to Ligny. Only when he realized the full extent of Napoleon's movements did he start to force-march through the Belgian countryside. He did not reach Ligny in time to influence the battle, had he done so Napoleon could have been beaten and Waterloo would have been a battle of considerably less importance. On 18 June, Bülow began to advance to Waterloo at dawn and started his attacks on Plancenoit at around 5.00 pm with only a portion of his Corps. The remainder were committed to the battle as they arrived on the scene. The ferocity of the battle in Plancenoit probably blinded Napoleon to the opportunity that Ney had created when the latter captured La Haie-Sainte.

Drouet, Jean-Baptiste, Comte d'Erlon 1765-1844

D'Erlon was an experienced officer who fought in all of Napoleon's campaigns, and commanded the ill-fated 1st Corps at Quatre Bras/Ligny and Waterloo. On 16 June, he countermarched between Quatre Bras and Ligny because he received conflicting orders, firstly from Napoleon via Soult, and then from an angry Ney who had not been informed of the initial order. Consequently, d'Erlon was not present at either battle where the presence of his Corps would have proved decisive. Tasked with what was planned to be the battle-winning assault on 18 June, his Corps was halted by Picton's Division before being brutally repulsed by the British heavy cavalry under Uxbridge. He valiantly regrouped and continued assaulting the Allied centre throughout the day, before being overwhelmed by the arrival of Ziethen's Corps. D'Erlon was part of a Bonapartist plot to stage a coup d'etat when Napoleon first escaped from Elba. For this action he was sentenced to death on the restoration of the Bourbon Monarchy. D'Erlon remained in exile, avoiding the fate that had been awarded to him until pardoned by Charles X in 1825. He was created a Marshal of France in 1843 at the age of 78.

Gneisenau, Augustus Wilhelm, Graf von Neithardt 1760-1831

Gneisenau was the Prussian Chief of Staff, a powerful position that effectively gave him dual control over the Army with Blücher and the ability to over-rule the latter if required. In essence, Gneisenau was a very competent officer and a model of Prussian efficiency and precision. His Achilles heel was his mistrust of the British, and Wellington in particular, that was created when Gneisenau accidentally came into possession of a secret letter at the Vienna Conference outlining a plan between Bourbon France, Austria and Britain to form an alliance against Prussia. Wellington had the misfortune to be Britain's representative in Vienna at the time. His mistrust of Wellington clouded Gneisenau's thinking after Ligny, where the former promised to support the Prussians with 20,000 men 'if I am not attacked myself'. Disregarding the fact that Wellington had been in action at Quatre Bras all day, Gneisenau believed that the Prussians were being left to the mercy of Napoleon, and was all for heading back to Prussia. That Blücher managed to persuade him otherwise meant that the Prussians withdrew to Wavre and were in a position to reinforce Wellington on 18 June. At Waterloo, Gneisenau took command of the pursuit that was conducted with such ferocity and violence that Napoleon had no chance of reorganizing his shattered army. Gneisenau went on to become a Field Marshal and the Governor of Berlin, before dying of cholera whilst on campaign in Poland.

Grouchy, Emmanuel, Marquis 1766-1847

Born into the pre-Revolution French aristocracy, Grouchy was a life-long cavalry officer whose first experience of all-arms command was the Waterloo campaign, for which he was created a Marshal. He was tasked by Napoleon after the inconclusive victory at Ligny to keep the Prussians from linking with Wellington, and was given one third of the army with which to achieve this task. He engaged only the Prussian III Corps under General Thielmann at Wavre, but believed he had trapped the main body of the Prussian force. He thus failied in his main task. He became aware of Napoleon's defeat on the morning of 19 June and faced a dilemma as to what to do next. He declined the option put forward by General Vandamme, one of the officers who had implored Grouchy to 'march to the guns' on 18 June, which involved capturing Brussels, forcing the allies to turn back from France. He successfully extracted his Corps to France in good order, available to fight with Napoleon as required. After the Bourbon restoration, Grouchy went into exile in Philadelphia and only returned to France once he had been pardoned.

Picton, Sir Thomas 1758-1815

In many ways, Picton came from the same mould as Ney: courageous, direct and loved by his soldiers, his career had begun as an Ensign at the age of thirteen. His reputation was made in the Peninsular War where he commanded the 'Fighting 3rd Division' and his presence during the Waterloo campaign was specifically requested by Wellington. Picton managed to lose his uniform during the journey to Belgium and fought the campaign in civilian clothes, complete with a rusty coloured top hat. His

Sir Thomas Picton, the beloved commander of the British 3th Infantry Division, was killed whilst leading his men from the front in defeating d'Erlon's assault. (Sir Martin Archer Shee)

divisional forced march over twenty-one miles to Quatre Bras ensured his troops arrived just in time to reinforce the desperately stretched Dutch-Belgian troops. The Division was heavily engaged throughout the day and most units suffered 35-50 per cent casualties. Picton was wounded in the hip during the battle, but as he was concerned that he would be invalided back to Brussels he told only his valet about the injury. As he led his troops forward to counter d'Erlon's Corps, Picton encouraged his men by calling them every insult imaginable in the language that the common soldier would understand. Struck by a bullet in his temple, he fell and never saw the repulse of the French that swung the battle into his commander's favour. Sir Thomas is buried at St Paul's Cathedral in London, next to Wellington's sarcophagus.

Soult, Nicholas, Jean de Dieu, Duke de Dalmatie 1769-1851

Soult remains one of the enigmas of the Napoleonic era. As a general he had a good reputation, despite being defeated by Wellington in the Peninsular War and having a known personality clash with Ney. His loyalties however are shrouded in mystery, and at best, it could be said that Soult was loyal only unto himself and incapable of writing clear and precise orders. After Napoleon's abdication in 1814, Soult became the Bourbon Minister for War, and was vocal in his denouncement of Napoleon's escape from Elba and his determination to see the former Emperor captured and executed. Amazingly, he was made Napoleon's Chief of Staff, but lacked Marshal Berthier's (his predecessor's) ability to put down clearly in writing the oft-rambling thoughts and plans of Napoleon. Orders, particularly to Ney, lacked a sense of urgency and requirement for immediate and aggressive action, something that Ney had specialized in during his violent career. Unlike Ney, d'Erlon and others, he was not hounded, arrested, tried for treason, exiled or executed. He was captured but paroled on the orders of the ultra-royalist Comte d'Artois. D'Artois had tried to assassinate Napoleon and had ordered the murder of Marshal Berthier, yet in Soult's justification of his return to Napoleon after the latter resumed as Emperor, he claimed d'Artois 'knew my mind'. Soult spent some time in Prussia in exile before being pardoned and reconciled with Louis XVIII. Were the orders to Ney deliberately vague because of his continuing dislike of the man, or was it part of a more sinister plot?

Uxbridge, Henry Paget, Earl of 1768-1854

Like Wellington, Uxbridge fought as an infantry colonel during the ill-fated campaign in Flanders in 1794 under the Duke of York. After the campaign, he transferred to the cavalry where he built his reputation in the harsh conditions of the Peninsular War. Bad blood existed between Wellington and Uxbridge because of an affair between the latter and the former's sister-in-law, resulting in two scandalous society divorces. Wellington requested Uxbridge not be sent as Cavalry Commander to Belgium, but the Duke of York, probably stung by the success of Wellington compared to his known incompetence, refused the request. His contribution to the outcome of the battle should not be underestimated. The timing of the charge he ordered by the Union and Household Brigades of heavy cavalry destroyed not only d'Erlon's Corps and Napoleon's plan of battle, but bought vital time for Wellington. Struck in the knee 'in the low ground beyond La Haie-Sainte, and perhaps a quarter of an hour before dusk', Uxbridge underwent amputation at the village of Waterloo with true cavalry flair. He seemed to appear 'not the least bit shaken' during the operation, and when it was over announced that 'I have been a beau these forty-seven years and it would not be fair to cut the young men out any longer.' His severed leg was buried in the garden of the house at which he underwent the operation, but was reunited with its owner when Uxbridge died. The prosthesis can be viewed in the Wellington Museum in Waterloo.

Ziethen, Hans Ernst Karl, Graf von 1770-1848

Ziethen's Corps was heavily involved in the action at Ligny, and then provided an expert rearguard action that allowed the Prussian army to regroup at Wavre. His troops were undoubtedly battle-weary and quite probably exhausted when the Corps was ordered to march to Waterloo.

On approaching the battlefield, Blücher ordered Ziethen's Corps to divert south to reinforce the attack on Plancenoit, but Ziethen realized the full extent of the crisis Wellington was facing in his centre. He ignored Blücher's order and arriving through Papelotte, cutting d'Erlon's Corps in half and creating panic in the French sector of the eastern edge of the battlefield. His timing was perfect as it coincided with the defeat of the Imperial Guard and instigated the start of the collapse of Napoleon's army. Ziethen and his men advanced into France with the rest of the Prussian Army and, following the final abdication of Napoleon, Ziethen became commander of the Prussian element of the Allied Army of Occupation.

APPENDIX C

EFFECTIVE STRENGTHS OF THE ARMIES ON THE BATTLEFIELD AT WATERLOO, 18 JUNE 1815

The relative strengths of the armies at Waterloo on the 18 June vary from source to source, and most are drawn from the initial strengths at the start of the campaign. This is misleading as it does not account for several factors that severely influenced the effective strengths. Grouchy was detached from the main body of the French Army with almost one third of Napoleon's total force, troops were detached from the battle strength to guard lines of communications and there are obviously the casualties sustained at Ligny and Quatre Bras to consider. The Prussians did not arrive on the battlefield simultaneously, and it was not until after 7.00 pm that their presence was decisive. Napoleon was ahead of his time in the use of 'All-Arms' groupings, placing infantry, cavalry and artillery in Corps groups; Wellington preferred to keep his troops in smaller packages that he often placed personally. The table below tries to account for the factors influencing the initial strengths of the armies involved, and cuts through the various and complex groupings that the different commanders chose to adopt. The table therefore breaks the troops down into categories rather than formations and uses time as a means to account for effective Prussian strength at Waterloo.

Table of Effective Strengths

	Infantry	*Cavalry*	*Artillery Engrs*	*Guns*	TOTAL
FRENCH	49,776	14,739	7,529	246	**72,044 + 246 guns**
ALLIED	49,608	12,408	5,645	156	**67,661 + 156 guns**
PRUSSIANS					
By 4.30 pm	12,043	2,720	1,143	64	**15,906 + 64 guns**
By 6.00 pm	25,381	2,720	1,143	64	**29,244 + 64 guns**
By 7.00 pm	41,283	8,858	1,803	104	**51,944 + 104 guns**

APPENDIX D

A REGIMENTAL EXPERIENCE

1ST (ROYAL SCOTS) REGIMENT OF FOOT IN THE WATERLOO CAMPAIGN

'Out of a company 100 strong on the morning of the 16th eleven now sat round to drink, not to the health, but to the memory of those who had vacated their places in the ranks'.
Private Douglas, 19 June 1815

The 3rd Battalion of the 1st (Royal Scots) Regiment of Foot was not unusual in its experience during the Waterloo campaign. Part of Sir Thomas Picton's Division, the battalion was heavily involved in the action at Quatre Bras as well as Waterloo itself. Casualties were 'normal' for 18 June, but were exaggerated by those sustained two days earlier. The 3rd Battalion contained relatively few veterans from the Peninsular War, but those present had fought in all the major battles of the war and would have offered an invaluable steadying influence.

After a twenty-one mile forced march, Picton's Division was immediately engaged on arrival at Quatre Bras. The 1st Regiment was required to bayonet charge a French infantry column, which it subsequently routed. As Ney increased the pressure on the Allied army holding the crossroads, cavalry from Kellerman's Corps charged the newly arrived infantry. The 1st Regiment was forced to form a square to repel the new threat and 'though charged for six or seven times by an infinite superiority of numbers, the French cavalry never for an instant made the slightest impression upon the square of The Royal Scots.'

Following the Allied withdrawal from Quatre Bras on the morning 17 June, the 1st Regiment formed up with the rest of General Sir Denis Pack's Brigade to the north of the fork in the road in the vicinity of the French memorial to the 21st Line Regiment (Appendix A, Memorial 23). As d'Erlon's attack reached the ridge, the Regiment was involved in the defeat of Marcognet's Division, the French 21st Line Infantry being amongst the troops involved. During the fight with Marcognet's Division, officers were falling fast, none quicker than those carrying the Colours. When Ensign Kennedy, carrying the King's Colour became the last Ensign to fall, a Sergeant tried to take his turn as bearer, but could not prise the young man's dead grasp from the staff. The Sergeant picked up Kennedy and carried both the body and the Colour rearward for safety and in an act of supreme chivalry a French Colonel restrained his troops from firing until the Sergeant was safe. Sergeant Major Quick then assumed the responsibility for bearing the King's Colour but was 'shot through the heart'. His name can be found alongside those of the officers who died at Quatre Bras and Waterloo on a commemorative plinth inside the church in the village of Waterloo. After the defeat of the French attack, the 1st Regiment resumed its position on the reverse of the slope, being cannonaded for several hours.

As the crisis of the battle approached, La Haie-Sainte fell to Ney at some stage between 6.00 and 6.30 pm. The resulting panic in the centre of the Allied line resulted in Wellington repositioning the brigade on the eastern edge of the Brussels road, half way between Mont St Jean farm and the crossroads. As the Imperial Guard was defeated, the 1st Regiment was given one final task, to recapture the farm complex of La Haie-Sainte, which it did at about 8.30 pm.

The 1st (Royal Scots) Regiment of Foot began the campaign with 604 all ranks and finished with 242. It is interesting to see how those casualties were spread across the three days as it shows that the intensity of the fighting was similar on both 16 and 18 June in respect of casualties. There is a difference of only 1 per cent between the battles of Quatre Bras and Waterloo in the percentage of casualties sustained, although the numbers of casualties sustained were higher at Quatre Bras. The overall figure of 60 per cent casualties for the three days of the campaign is

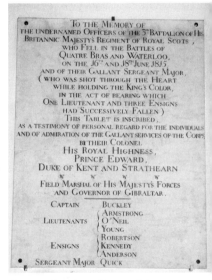

Memorial to the officers of the 1st (Royal Scots) Regiment of Foot killed during the Waterloo campaign. The Regimental experience was not unusual for Picton's Division. During the battles of Quatre Bras and Waterloo the Regiment suffered sixty per cent casualties and only nine of their forty-three officers remained unscathed.

standard for the regiments that formed Picton's Division and were not outrageous compared to other infantry regiments in the Allied army. Of note is the wide difference between the numbers of those killed and wounded. In general, the ratio between dead and wounded was at least

		Officers	Soldiers	Total	%(Rounded)	
QUATRE BRAS	In Line	43	561	604	100%	In Line
	Killed	6	20	26	4	16 June
	Wounded	12	180	192	32	
WATERLOO	In Line	25	361	386	100%	In Line
	Killed	2	13	15	4	18 June
	Wounded	14	115	129	33	
CAMPAIGN	In Line	9	233	242	40%	In Line
	Killed	8	33	41	7	19 June
	Wounded	26	295	321	53	

1:4, and at Waterloo was 1:6 in the Allied army. The 1st Regiment has a ratio of nearly 1:8. However, many of those, particularly on 18 June, would have been wounded by artillery and would have required subsequent amputation, with the high mortality rate from disease that invariably followed. It was standard practice at that time for any wound to a limb involving a joint, or anything more substantial than a simple fracture or flesh wound to be amputated at the earliest opportunity.

The fact that only nine officers did not become casualties shows that 79 per cent of the Regiment's officers were either killed or wounded. When compared with the figure of 58 per cent casualties amongst the soldiers it is an indication of the officer corps' role at the time. Officers, especially junior and middle-ranking regimental officers, were expected to encourage the soldiers with acts of extreme bravery. The high percentage of officer casualties suffered by the 1st Regiment would suggest those concerned performed the duty expected of them. The fact that they were only armed with a light sword indicated that officers were not expected to form an efficient part of the killing machine. If figures were available to show the percentage of enemy killed by officers compared with soldiers, it would probably be below 1 per cent. (the officer contingent in the battalion was 8 per cent).

After the battle, the 1st (Royal Scots) Regiment of Foot advanced to Paris where it formed part of the Allied Army of Occupation, returning to Britain in 1817.

APPENDIX E

BIBLIOGRAPHY

DE CHAIR *Napoleon on Napoleon*
    Brockhampton Press 1992
CHANDLER David *Napoleon's Marshals*
    Macmillan Publishing Company
DELDERFIELD Ronald *Napoleon's Marshals*
    Cooper Square Press 1962
DE POTTER Jean-Pierre *Mise à Mort de L'Empire par Napoléon*
    Editions Graffiti, 1981
FITCHETT WH *The Great Duke*
    Smith, Elder & Co. 1911
RINGS Jean H *Dictionnaire de la bataille de Waterloo*
    Les Guides 1815, 1995
HAMILTON-WILLIAMS David *Waterloo – New Perspectives. The Great Battle Reappraised*
    Brockhampton Press, 1993
HASTINGS Max *Military Anecdotes*
    Oxford University Press, 1985
HAYTHORNTHWAITE Philip *Napoleon: The Final Verdict*
    Arms & Armour Press 1996
HOWARTH David *Waterloo, A Near Run Thing*
    Collins, 1968
KEEGAN John *The Face of Battle*
    Penguin, 1976
LOGIE Jacques - *L'évitable défaite*
    Editions Duculot, 1984
PAGET Julian & SAUNDERS Derek *Hougoumont, The Key To Victory At Waterloo*
    Leo Cooper, Pen & Sword Books, 2001
PERICOLI Ugo *1815, The Armies At Waterloo*
    Sphere Books, 1973
PERRETT Bryan *Last Stand*
    Arms & Armour Press, 1991

PERRETT Bryan *Against All Odds*
Arms & Armour Press, 1999
RINGS Jean H *Dictionnaire de la bataille de Waterloo*
Les Guides 1815, 1995
ROBERTS Andrew *Napoleon and Wellington*
Les Guides 1815, 1995
SIBORNE Captain William *History Of The Waterloo Campaign*
Weidenfeld & Nicholson 2001
SPEECKAERT Georges & BACKER Isabelle *Les 135 vestiges et Monuments Commemoratifs des Combats de 1815 en Belgique*
Action & Recherche Culturelles, Brabant
TASQUIN René *Le Champs de Bataille de Waterloo, Pas à Pas*
Editions Interprint, Brussels
WELLER Jac *Wellington At Waterloo*
Greenhill Books, 1992
YOUNG Peter H *Napoleon's Marshals*
Osprey Publishing Limited 1973

Index